A BIBLICAL PERSPECTIVE

THE
Christian
FAMILY

DR. EUGENE SHERMAN

Copyright © 2022 by Dr. Eugene Sherman.

ISBN 978-1-64133-749-6 (softcover)
ISBN 978-1-64133-750-2 (ebook)

All rights reserved. No part of this book may be reproduced or transmitted in any form or by any means, electronic or mechanical, including photocopying, recording, or by any information storage and retrieval system without express written permission from the author, except in the case of brief quotations embodied in critical reviews and certain other noncommercial uses permitted by copyright law.

Printed in the United States of America.

Brilliant Books Literary
137 Forest Park Lane Thomasville
North Carolina 27360 USA

Contents

Dedication v
Preface vii
Rationale for the Subject ix
Acknowledgment xi
Introduction xiii

Chapter 1:   The Christian family 1
Chapter 2:   Statuses in the Christian family 4
Chapter 3:   An Ordinary Praying Man 7
Chapter 4:   The Good Father 10
Chapter 5:   The Righteous Father 13
Chapter 6:   The Biased Father 17
Chapter 7:   The Grieving Yet Praying Father 20
Chapter 8:   Father Knows Best 24
Chapter 9:   The Dilemma of Motherhood 28
Chapter 10: The Praying Mother 33
Chapter 11: The Prevailing Mother 37
Chapter 12: The Overzealous Mother 41
Chapter 13: The Sacrificing Mother 44
Chapter 14: The Altruistic Mother 48

Chapter 15: Knowing Your Whereabouts 52
Chapter 16: The Young Dreamer..55
Chapter 17: The Haughty Son 58
Chapter 18: The Children of Light..62
Chapter 19: The Toils and Rewards of Study....................................66
Chapter 20: Obedience: Its Obligations and Rewards.......................69
Chapter 21: Benefits of Obedient Children 72
Chapter 22: The Frazzled Sister 76
Chapter 23: The spiritual values of grandparents..............................80
Chapter 24: Facing Life 84

Epilogue..87
Sources..89
About The Author..90

Dedication

This book is dedicated to memories of my late parents, Deacon Eugene Sherman, Sr. and Sister Mary Martin Sherman, along with my siblings: Frank (deceased), James (deceased), Larry, Eunice, and Nadine. Additionally, it includes my beloved wife, Dr. Dolores E Sherman, who departed to be with the Lord on December 15, 2008, after thirty-nine years if blissful marriage. Dolores and I had no children.

Preface

This book is a compilation of several lectures undergirded by the common theme of the Christian family. It makes no attempt to assert that Christianity is the only, or even best, form of family life. However, it is asserted that the Christian family's format is consistent with the New Testament teachings on family life. The epilogue of this study contains expanded dimensions of the Christian Family. While this document on the Christian family is anchored by New Testament, it does recognize and utilize the Old Testament account of creation in which the term *wife* is recorded in Genesis 3:20— "And Adam called his wife's name Eve because she was the mother of all living." While there were some monogamous (*one husband and one wife*) units in Old Testament history, there were many examples of polygynous (one husband and more than one wife) during that historical era.

It must be noted, however, that firm teachings on family life were part of the Old Testament. An eclectic overview includes the following: Jacob obeyed his father and mother (Gen.28:7); "Honor thy father and thy mother; that thy days may be long upon the land which the Lord giveth thee" (Ex.20:12); "Train up the child in the way he should go and when he is old, he will not depart from it" (Pr.22:6); and "Her children arise up and call her blessed; her husband also, and he praiseth her" (Pr. 31:28).

In sum, this collection of sermons on the Christian family was name in keeping with the New Testament foundation used to undergird both the title and the sermons. Additionally, it is in the New Testament that Jesus obeyed his mother and worked in his foster father's carpentry shop. Later in his ministry, Jesus was involved in solving medical problems with a family context, consoling Martha and Mary over the death of their brother, Lazarus. Within another setting, Jesus used the prodigal son to illustrate the readiness of the Father to receiving penitent sinner who returned to him. Lastly, He promised that He was going away to prepare a place where the believers could ever be with the Lord. Within this context, the New Testament presents Jesus as the ultimate groom and the Church as the bride for the eternal consummation in heaven—the ultimate Christian family.

Rationale for the Subject

An historical concern about the nature of human social organization led to some consensus that there are five majors' components, especially in Western society. The components were labeled as social institutions and placed into five categories that included the following: religion, family, education, economy, and government. This classification continues to be viable in this twenty-first century; however, additional units have been identified, two of which are the military complex and the scientific establishment.

While each of these institutions—a term that denotes a concept and a structure—performs a network of functions necessary for societal welfare. One of them, the family, is the focus of this book. This institution personifies innumerable functions essential for the maintenance and existence of humankind. Two of the critical ones are procreation of children and stabilization of adult personality. The family, as an institution, is found throughout the world although its structure may vary by factors that include the following: number of spouse(s) permitted, source of authority, residency of the newlywed, and faith group/denomination of the couple. Of special emphasis for this book is the religious anchor known as Christianity; hence, the title is *The Christian Family*. This anchor avoids any assessment of other religious perspectives and concentrates on the Christian family as depicted in the Holy Bible.

Acknowledgment

Words of appreciation are extended to innumerable persons, including my professors of sociology, history, and gerontology in undergraduate and graduate schools; my seminary professors; the students in my classes during a thirty-five-year tenure at Albany State University (GA) and Bethany Theological Seminary in Dothan, AL; the members of Institutional First Baptist Church in Albany, GA, where I am foundering pastor (1971–Present); and the readers of sermons/lectures on www.biblicalechoes.com.

Introduction

Both biblical and secular accounts concur that some form of human arrangement existed for making and/or reproduction. The Bible traces this form of interaction back to the period of creation. It is recorded in Genesis—"took a rib from Adam, made he a woman, and brought her unto the man" (Gen.2:22). Adam, according the Bible, "called his wife's name's Eve, because she was the mother of all living" (Gen.3:20). After this union between Adam and Eve was blessed with the son, Cain, later, a second son was born; his name was Abel. The birth of Abel created a social union known as the family because it consisted of parents and at least one child. This configuration later became accepted as the definition of the traditional family. Later in this introduction, the concepts of family types and functions will be discussed. At the present, however, attention will be focused on some anthropological research that warrant concluding that both primitive mankind and the lower animal world evolved methods of mating—some for short periods and others for long duration—for reproduction. Westermarck, a Finnish sociologists and philosopher, wrote extensively on the evolution. Noting the practice of female animals and birds to attract the attention of their male counterpart, Westermarck concluded that the behavior of primitive man followed a similar pattern. Since he observed that the male tended to establish some permanency with the female after the birth of offspring. Westermarck asserted that the first family was patriarchal, or father controlled.

In sharp contrast to Westermarck, the Swedish anthropologist Bachofen asserted that the female bird, animal, and human all possessed subtle methods for attracting their male counterpart, but they never yielded to being controlled by the male. Bachofen's view is presented in his book *Das Mutterrecht*. He, therefore, concluded that the original human family structure was a matriarch, or mother controlled.

An examination of the research on family power structure clearly shows the preponderance of patriarchal family form throughout the evolution of humanity. The lone exception was the period of slavery in America from the 1619-1863. Within the context of the system, an array of practices emerged, to name but a few: marriage between slaves were seldom encouraged, and slave women were bred with a slave stallion to produce a herculean offspring who would eventually be a "good" plantation worker or an ideal person for sale at the slave market. Added to this plantation-controlled sexuality of the female slaves were the frequent instances in which the plantation owner, his son, or hired white worker would have sexual encounters with slave women irrespective of their desires. There was another type of sexual arrangement involving a slave man and a slave woman; it was the semblance of marriage. The event required permission from the plantation owner who would conduct the so-called wedding ceremony by having the two individuals to hold hands together and jump over a broomstick. Admittedly, such arrangement was fragile, for they could be ended by a decision to sell the male or female. Another ever present was the female's freedom to report marital problems to the plantation owner. Some residues of that mentality continue to exist in contemporary twenty-first-century America, especially in the rural South.

Having to provide an eclectic account of the evolution of family life, the focus will now be directed to another facet of family life. It is that of a multiplicity of concepts and practices centered on and/or impacting family life.

- Family structure by marital status—this category includes single, married, widowed, divorced, and separated. Added to this traditional list are common law marriage, serial cohabitation, and renting partners.
- Family structure by historical definition-this category encompasses the following: the traditional family-i.e., husband, wife, and at least one child; the nontraditional, known as single-parent family, i.e., an arrangement consisting of a parent with its child or children; and the same sex entity that consists of two

persons with a common gender that may or not include a child or children; the extended family that includes three generations, such as a grandparent, parent(s), and at least one child.

- The blended family, which is one in which the couple each brings at least one child into the marriage; and finally, the foster family created by a court order living arrangement within a setting in which the child or children is/are usually not related to the adult providing the living arrangement.

- Family structure by number of spouse(s) permitted. Under this topic, the following forms of marriage exist: monogamy—one man and one woman; this is the legal form of marriage in the United States of America; polygamy—one man and several wives, a form of marriage practiced in America by the founder of Mormonism; it has since declared to be a variance with the American marital code. However, during its era, the founder was described in the following quote. Brigham Young was perhaps the most famous polygynous of the early Latter-Day Saints Movement, marrying a total of fifty-five wives, fifty-four of them after becoming a Latter-Day Saint. He stated that upon being taught about plural marriage," It was the first time in my life that I desired the grave." "By the time of his death, Young had fifty-seven children by sixteen of his wives; forty-six of his children reached adulthood "(Firefox). It should be noted, however, that members of that group are now monogamous. Another form of marriage is known as polyandry, a term that refers to a form of marriage in which a woman is the wife of two or more men at the same time. It is found in some areas of Tibet and India. Lastly, there is a form of marriage known as group marriage. It is an arrangement" of several men with several women. As an institutionalized social practice, group marriage is extremely rare.; nowhere does it appear to have. "

- Next, there is the marriage structure based upon the method of determining lineage. Generally, the American is patrilineal—tracing descent through the father's family name. While embracing this procedure, many females are choosing to keep their maiden name and adding the family name of the husband.

- Lastly, there is the marriage structure based on the commonality of variation in demographics; this analysis of structure includes two terms: *endogamy and exogamy*. The first term denotes the practice of selecting a mate from within demographic boundaries of both individuals; it includes the same race, religion, social class, educational attainment to mention but a few of the obvious variables. *Exogamy*, in contrast, refers to a setting in which the mates have different demographics, for example, an inter-racial couple. As cultural diversity becomes more wide-spread, it seems tenable to conclude that exogamous marriages will increase. Against this historical discussion of some dimensions of family life, the cogent question now becomes what is meant by the *Christian family*? Instead of giving an operational definition of the Christian family, the emphasis will be placed on a general discussion of the Christian family. It is, first, an entity that embraces the Judeo-Christian creed; it accepts the Bible as the Word of God penned by holy men of old as they were moved by the Spirit of God; it believes in the doctrine of total depravity; it accepts the finished work of Jesus; it believes that salvation is acceptable to anyone who complies with Romans 10:9; it embraces monogamy—one spouse—as the Christian form of marriage; it obligates parents to train up the children the way they should go; it teaches that children should obey their parents; it emphasizes religious (Christian) training, regular worship as taught in Hebrews 10: 25; and it accepts the frequently posted wall decor-the family that prays together stays together.

Chapter 1

The Christian family

> And, ye fathers, provoke not your children to wrath...Children, obey your parents in the Lord for this is right.
>
> —Ephesians 6–4.1

The family is one of five basic institutions found in most societies. Its origin can be traced back to the Book of Genesis. Therein is found the narrative of God's creation of man (Adam), woman (Eve), and later two sons: Cain and Abel. After the murder of Abel, "Adam knew his wife again; and she bare a son, and called his name Seth" (Gen.4:24).

The original family conformed to a pattern known as the traditional family, term that denotes father, mother, and at least one child. Over the years, several different titles have been and are being used to denote family life. Some of these designations are the following: the single parent family, i.e., the absence of one parent— usually the father; the extended family, which is one consisting of grandparents, parents, and children; and the broken family, one in which a parent is permanently removed by divorce, incarceration.

In view of the vital role that family life plays in both personal and societal stability, the sermon today-in keeping with our Annual Family Worship Service-has been entitled" The Christian Family". It will seek to exalt family unity and encourage family members to heed, biblical principles in their relationships. The sermon, differing from the threefold points of analysis, will today encompass four lines of inquiry, namely: functions of the family, basic forms of family types, biblical teaching on family devotion, and outcomes from proper family religious training.

Having earlier given a background sketch on the family, attention will now be directed to the inquiries listed above, the first one being functions of the family. Initially, the union consists of husband and wife. Within that context, the functions are twofold. The first is that of stabilizing the adults' personalities within an approved social setting, which is marriage rather than a promiscuous union that can include shacking of two unmarried persons or patronizing houses of ill repute.

The second function of the married couple is that of pro creating and rearing children. When the couple starts a family, it opens the doorway for approximately eighteen years of obligations. This list of obligations is extensive; however, four of the more prominent ones are the following: religious training, a topic to be further developed later in this sermon; the economic function that includes food, clothing, shelter, medical, an allowance, and nowadays, a" ride"; the education that encompasses pre-K through college and, in many instances, after college the youngsters return home to get "jump-started "in the world of work; lastly, there is the governance function in which parents are assumed to be the major decision makers within the family.

Beloved, there are many other functions associated with child rearing. Suffice it to hear that indicate, however, that the proper fulfillment of four functions just discussed will enhance normal child growth and development within the context of a harmonious family setting.

Having explored some functions of the family attention, we will now be focused on forms of types of families. The family sociologists have coined to terms to describe the historic American family; those terms are *Eurocentric and Afrocentric*. The first terms are applied to the Caucasian(white) group, and it denotes a family style in which both parents are in the home, the husband is gainfully employed, and the mother's primary role is that of caring for the children and fulfilling household responsibilities. The Afrocentric family style, in contrast, is used to characterize the black population in America. As depicted therein, the Afrocentric family is often of the single-parent type, the mother is gainfully employed, the source of family finance, and prone to become a victim of abuse. While there are some differences between the Eurocentric and Afrocentric family styles, both of them have a common biblical obligation to promote family devotion. In support of this assertion, a few parental obligations will be specified. Parents must introduce their children to religious training within the home. Ephesians 6:4 calls upon fathers to "bring them [children]up in the nurture and admonition of the Lord." St. Paul referenced the value of early religious training in the life of Timothy; thus, he wrote, "And from a child thou hast known the Holy Scripture" (2 Timothy 3:15). In his first letter to the people of Thessalonica, Paul's call emphasized the need for daily prayer. Thus, he penned, "In everything give thanks: for this is the will of God in Christ Jesus concerning you "(1st The. 5: 18). This scriptural admonition is a call for parents to teach their children to give thanks for their life and daily experiences.

Beloved, if parents heed these scriptures in their efforts to promote family devotions, they can anticipate and will receive bountiful blessings. This fact leads to the final consideration of the sermon, which are outcomes from early and continuous family devotionals. Although they are many, only four of them will be presented herein. First, the child will become properly focused religiously. "Train up the child in the way he should go: and when he is old, he will not depart from it" (Prov.22:6). Secondly, the child will learn to respect its parents. "Honor thy father and thy mother that thy days will be long upon the land thy giveth thee". (Exodus 20:12). Thirdly, the child in later years will bring much joy to its parent(s)." Correct thy son, and he will give thee rest; yea, he will give the light unto thy soul" (Prov. 29:17).

Lastly, what can a mother expect from devotional training of her children? My friends, the Bible has an encouraging answer; it states, "Her children arise up and call her blessed" (Prov. 31:28).

In closing, this family day worship sermon entitled "The Christian Family" was planned to extol the value of family devotion as an ongoing process. It submitted biblical rather than philosophical or even psychological principles. In sum, the sermon is a call for a prayer as an element in the family life and to rekindle the challenge contained in the words of the song, "Family Prayer," where the plea is beamed "don't forget the family prayer."

Chapter 2

Statuses in the Christian family

People are classified by institutions and statuses. In this book, the institutions are family, religion, education, government, economics. The statuses (or positions) are father, mother, child, and grandparent(s). The totality of and interaction among people within these statuses give rise to a structure known as the family. Obviously, there are family structures that embrace different religious, ethnic, national, and even atheistic ideologies. However, this book about the family that understands, embraces, and seeks to govern itself consistent with Christian principles and percepts. Hence this book was entitled *The Christian Family: A Biblical Perspective*. Its contents were arranged in accordance with the order in which the selected statuses occurred in the evolution of human kind.

The Father

The word *father* denotes a masculine individual who has procreated himself. He is a provider, defender, arbitrator, and highly visible in the family. The father, further, provides motivation, direction, and encouragement for the family. When needed, the father administers discipline within biblical and legal guideline. Hopefully the father embraces Paul's teaching regarding fatherly obligations that include "And ye fathers, provoke not your children not to wrath, but bring them up in the nurture and admonition of the Lord "(Eph.6:4). Chapters 4 through 8 address some aspects of being a father.

The Mother

The word *mother* refers to a female who has given birth to a child. She is responsible for the total nurture of the infant. Her numerous roles include feeding, bathing, clothing, cleansing and caring for its place of sleep. The mother provides the initial experiences in the social training (smiling, talking playing and uttering words— all of which are necessary) required for the biological infant to eventually become an increasingly competent person.

In addition to the child-bearing and rearing process, the mother is overseer of the family household. In this capacity, the mother prepares the meals, supervises and cares for the children's clothes, monitors the homework activities provides leadership in ethical and religious training, offers comfort and encouragement for the children, instills goals and encourages pursuit of them, and tends to place herself at the end of the daily chores.

The mother is viewed as being compassionate, dedicated, a near-endless worker. She rejoices in the social, educational, religious and maturation of her children. Hopefully, in return, "her children arise up, and called her blessed; her husband also, and he praiseth her" (Prov.31:23) Chapter 9 through 14 center on some aspects of motherhood.

The Child

The child is a product of cohabitation of a male and a female. From the Christian anchor, this activity should have occurred within a marriage. Sadly, there are numerous births in which the male and female is not married. Thus, the child is labeled as being in a single- parent home. The choice of its own, the child is subjected to inequities and even hostilities by its schoolmates, neighbors, decision makers, and numerous individuals with its socio-cultural network.

Hopefully, the child will, nonetheless, acquire a positive outlook on life instead of falling into delinquent lifestyle. The child is expected to be obedient, respectful, helpful with household chores, cordial toward people, truthful, embrace, principles of Christianity, goal oriented toward adulthood and employment, and embrace Paul's teaching, "When I was a child, I spoke as a child, I understand as a child, I thought as a child, but when I became a man, I put away childless things" (1st Cor. 13:11) Chapters 16 through 21 embody teachings on being a child.

The Grandmother

The grandmother is a female who is mother either of a child's mother or father. She often lives away from the mother and child, father and child, or parent and child. Owing to differences in longevity, the grandmother is more prevalent than the grandfather. The grandmother is becoming increasingly visible in many households, especially in the single-parent families. Within that setting, she is often a major player in the family setting. She may be cook, financer, motivator, disciplinarian, religious leader, babysitter, and caregiver. She was referenced by the Apostle Paul in one of his messages to Timothy; he wrote, "When I call to remembrance the unfeigned faith that is in thee, which dwelt first in thy grandmother Lois, and thy Eunice; and I am persuaded that in thee also" (2nd Tim. 1:3). The single-parent chapter (22) is devoted to the value of the grandparent in the family setting.

Chapter 3

An Ordinary Praying Man

James 5:16-18 and I Kings Chapters 17–18

The American calendar has four Sundays in which some aspects of family life is emphasized; those observations include Mother's Day—the second Sunday in May; Youth Day—the second Sunday in June; Father's Day—the third Sunday in June; and Grandparent's Day—the second Sunday in September. it is of interest to note that the occurrence of these days seems to reflect the emphasis placed on the individual or individuals. Thus, the most sentimental of these observations is Mother's Day while the least extolled one is Grandparent's Day. In between those two days are Youth and Father's Day with more focus on the youth than on the fathers. Although the Bible carries father orientation and the American nation exalt the role of fatherhood, the fact remains that the training and nurturing processes are largely performed by the mothers.

Of particular interest to the women, however, is the changing pattern in child-rearing; it is one of more involvement of the father with the chores of family life. Indications are that this trend will become more widespread as the economic demands require employment of both parents. On the gloomy side, it should be indicated that the unemployment of minority American males is creating a near role reversal in which the man must become the housekeeper.

While all members of the family should be committed to the practice of prayer, it is a sad fact to acknowledge that the father is most likely to be the non-prayer in the family. Our sermon, in this connection, has been planned to encourage fathers to develop— if not already established—a fervent belief in and practice of prayer. Oh! It is highly possible that some fathers, because of their low esteem in the family, are inclined to feel that they can make little, if any, difference in the family.

Additionally, such fathers may well believe that they are just ordinary persons and, therefore, unlike the praying biblical fathers, they are unable to accomplish much through prayer. Our sermon will beget this attitude of helplessness by reminding us of a prominent Old Testament personality, Elijah, who was described by James- in our text—as a man with our nature. This assertion is particularly relevant to contemporary times, for there is a tendency to think that Moses, Joshua, and Elijah were successful in their prayer life because they were extraordinary men. But a closer look in the Bible discloses that God does not seek extraordinary persons to do great things; rather, he takes ordinary people and helps them to do extraordinary things. In this regard, we are all ordinary people- especially the fathers—but God is waiting to do extraordinary things through us. Accordingly, let all of us make a commitment to allow God to use us to do extraordinary things for our family and others.

In helping us to be used by God, the sermon will address three steps and all of them concern some aspect of the word *pray*. They are the following: pray, pray with a clean heart, and pray in according with God's will. As background to the analysis of these three concerns, attention will be placed on the word *pray*. As a verb, *pray* is an admonition to petition God through utterance or silence. It also denotes the act of making a request in humble manner. To pray is further, the act of putting prayer into motion; hence, the admonition to pray means to commence some effort to commune with God while to be praying signifies that intent is being actualized. Against this belief discussion of the word *pray*, let us now turn attention to the first concern of our text; it is word *pray*.

In James 1:17, we are reminded that Elijah was a man just like men of today: in frailty and weakness. Do we, as men—especially—find it hard to pray? So did Elijah, but he prayed! Do we ever get discouraged? So did Elijah, but he prayed. Do we ever grow weary? So did Elijah, but he prayed. Elijah did not make excuses; rather, he prayed. So should we. Friends, throughout this Letter of James, we are all exhorted to pray: when we need wisdom, when we are suffering, when we are tempted, before we speak, when we are sick, and as we approach the end of life, we should be prayerful. Do we live this way? We are ordinary people, but through us, God can do extraordinary things.

Let us now turn to the second concern of Elijah's prayer. it is the admonition to pray with a clean heart (James 16). Elijah is given as a "righteous man," whose prayer is powerful and effective. James is not herein contending that Elijah has attained sinless perfection, but he was rather aware of and sought the nearness to God. Beloved, when we repent of our sins and place out faith and trust in Jesus Christ, He transfers His perfect righteousness to us; remember Abraham was righteous because he believed God? Fathers, do we trust God, have we trusted God, or will you trust God? In order to so trust God and be effective when we pray, let us always remember that we must pray with a clean heart. Friends, the secret for this mind-set is found in the Lord's Prayer— "forgive us of our sins and transgression as we so forgive others."

Thirdly and finally, as ordinary people we must pray in accordance with God's will (I King 17:2 and 18:1). These references describe God's message to Elijah regarding the drought and the rain. Even though the idea of prolonged drought might have worried Elijah, he nonetheless prayed for God's will to be done on earth. What about us? It is highly probable that we do not always know God's will in our life. There are some things, however, that God has instructed us to include in our prayer; they include overcoming temptation, to be patient, and to be a bold witness. But there are experiences of which we have no knowledge that awaits us and for which we have no solution. But thanks be to God who holds the future in his hands, there is an answer to all life's problems and mysteries.

Friends, as we pray, let us do so in the full knowledge that God always answers prayer! Sometimes, it is yes; sometimes, it is no, and sometimes, it is wait! So, as we fathers wait on God, let us not become disheartened as did Elijah when he fled to the cave.

Chapter 4

The Good Father

> Father, give me the portion of goods that falleth to me.
>
> —Luke 15:13

Father's Day is the third of four family-oriented Worship Sundays each year. Within the United States, it is celebrated the third Sunday in June. "Father's Day is a celebration honoring fathers and celebrating fatherhood, paternal bonds, and the influence of fathers in society." In keeping with this tradition, the worship for today will focus on fatherhood. The sermon, in this connection, has been entitled "The Good Father." It will encompass four instead of the usual three dimensions of the subject, namely: a definition and types of fathers, expectations of a father, the prodigal son's father, and our access to the Heavenly Father.

The scriptural background for our sermon was lifted from Luke 15 in which we find the account of the Pharisees who, in the usual manner, murmured and criticized Jesus for interacting with sinners. Jesus used the occasion to teach about access to and forgiveness by the Heavenly Father. He used three examples of the lost: a sheep, ten pieces of silver, and a (prodigal) son. Of particular interest for the sermon is the narrative of the younger son with his father. This relationship will be presented later in the sermon.

Against this scriptural anchor, attention will now be focused on the earlier specified components of the sermon, which is the definition and types of fathers. The word *father* denotes a male who has cause a female to have a child. Such a male is known as the father of procreation. Three other types of fathers are the following: the stepfather who marries a female who already has a child or children; the godfather is a male who assumes a measure of guardianship for a child; and the foster father who is usually authorized by the court to assume responsibilities for a child. The position of father carries an array of duties and responsibilities. Among the obligations are provisions for food, closing, and shelter, guidance and protection, motivation, inspiration, discipline, training that include for home life, school life, community life, religious life, career options, and being a mentor. Admittedly, this list is long but not exhaustive, yet, there are fathers who vary in the extent to which they seek to effectively fulfill their responsibilities.

There is a person who fulfilled these expectations, and his life is the next pivot of concern, which is the story of the prodigal son. While Luke's description of the prodigal episode does not give an economic profile of the father, his account does embody features from which certain conclusions are plausible. First, he was respected because the son referred to him as father; next, he was prosperous and this the son knew; hence, he asked for this portion of goods to which he was entitled; and he knew that his father would honor his request. The father made no demands, asked no questions and gave no advice. Instead, he merely issued to the son that to which he was entitled, but that is not the entire story! The son left the home, foolishly used his substance with riotous living, and soon he was broke. At that time trouble arose, a famine occurred and no one would give him anything to eat. He commenced to beg, and one person sent him to feed the swine. Remember that the Jewish people have a disdain for pork. The Bible says that he almost ate with the swine but came to himself; he remembered the hired servants back home, the abundance of food, and said unto himself, "I will arise and go to my father, and will say unto him, Father, I have sinned against heaven and before thee."

Oh, beloved, the narrative shows that the father saw him from far off, and when the son arrived, the father accepted him; but that is not all of the warm receptions—that is left to encourage you to read the fifteenth chapter of Luke. Fourthly and finally, the soul-searching question for each of us today is, do we know our Heavenly Father is watching over us? Have we ever, like the prodigal son, left the tenets of our faith? Are we inclined to do or say in appropriate things or words? If the answer is yes to these or other questions of deviation, let's remember to facts: First, like the Apostle Paul in Romans (17: 14-25), we are both carnal and spiritual, and often, there is a dilemma going on in us like we know what is right, but we are prone to do what is wrong. And secondly, when we discover and acknowledge that we have been devious, like the prodigal son, let us leave the swine and return to the Heavenly Father who already sees us and is anxiously waiting our return home where he can cleanse us of our iniquities, place new garments of forgiveness on our body, and give us manna for our spiritual nutrition. Oh! What a good father we have not only this day but for the rest of our earthly sojourn as well.

Amen and Happy Father's Day.

Chapter 5

The Righteous Father

> Blessed is the man that feareth the Lord…wealth and riches shall be in his house…and his righteousness endureth forever.
>
> —Psalm 112:1.3

America is a nation saturated with numerous and often contradictory values. Ideally, it professes to believe in God, especially on the weekend. At the same time, however, this nation is driven by economic forces. America, in this regard, strives to display religious commitment while embellishing materialistic goals. The sort of purge its citizens' conscience, this nation has set aside holidays, some of which include special worship Sundays. Our worship today will commemorate one of those special worship Sundays. The referenced service is that of Father's Day. The sermon has been entitled "The Righteous Father."

As a slight departure from the threefold analysis, this sermon will include four characteristics of the righteous father, namely: his place in his home; his relationship with his family members; his obligations to the family; and his role is a spiritual leader in the family. As a background for the sermon, attention is called the two of the words that anchor the message; they are *father* and *righteous*. Since the first word will run throughout the sermon; a brief definition is submitted at this time. Accordingly, *father* denotes a male who has reproduced himself through a sexual encounter with a female. Ideally, the female should be his wife, but the sad reality is that this type of relationship is becoming the exception rather than the rule. The next word *righteous* will be discussed in greater details. As noted in Vines *Expository Dictionary of Biblical Words*, this word can be used as a noun, a verb and an adverb. Without elaborating on those different contexts, the focus here is that of being righteous. Within this framework, righteousness embodies all that God expects of His people. The verbs associated with righteousness indicate the practicality of this concept. One judges, deals, sacrifices, and acts righteously. Additionally, it entails one who learns, teaches, and pursues after righteous ways. The Old Testament saints understood and embraced the precepts of righteousness, and they, therefore, asked God to deal righteously with a king as noted in Psalm 72:1 where it is recorded, "Give the king thy judgment O God, and thy righteousness unto the king's son." This and many other biblical references to righteous can be reduced to thinking and responding in a moral ethical, and compassionate manner. In this regard, the righteous father must be a man whose thoughts and actions are acceptable by God and beneficial to his offspring.

Against this background on the words *father* and *righteous*, let us not return to the earlier specified concerns about righteous father, the first of which is his place in the home. Closely related to the place is that of the father's position in home. From the biblical perspective, the father's position is that of head of the household. Within this setting, the father is to be respected as leader of the family. His responsibilities include arbitrator in family disputes, reconciler in emotional realities, disciplinarian in cases involving transgression, and a pavilion of defense against external forces that threaten the family.

The second inquiry regarding the righteous father is that all of his relationships with the family members. Beloved, the Bible entails numerous teachings on this topic. The righteous father can find clear guidelines for family interactions in Ephesians 5:23 where it is recorded, "Husbands, love your wives, even as Christ also loved the church, and gave himself for it." Continuing in verse 28, Paul wrote, So, ought men to love their wives as their own bodies. He that loveth his wife loveth himself."

The righteous father is also called upon to love his children. Ephesians 6:4 calls upon the fathers to "provoke not your children to wrath: but bring them up in the nurture and admonition of the Lord."

The righteous father, thirdly, has obligations through his family. Friends, this is the most frequent area of neglect for many men who wear the father title. Prior to examining scriptures and social expectations regarding fatherly obligations, a brief sidelight will be given to some devious father types. There is the procreator father who is a man who spreads or reproduces himself indiscriminately, publicizes his outside children, provides little, if any, support for the children, and is constantly looking for new avenues to exploit. The next devious father, is known as the pie-back father. He is the one who reclines in a household where the unmarried woman works and or receives entitlement benefits. He eats with the family, spend her money, and eyes the maturing young females in the household. He is of no financial benefit to the family, little emotional benefit to the woman, and a potential danger to the children. Beloved, there are many other devious fathers, but in the interest of time, the emphasis must return to the third concern of the righteous father; it is that of his obligations to the family.

The Holy Bible teaches that the righteous family must assume economic responsibility for his children. Thus, it raises the question as to what father "if his child ask bread will give him a stone and if he asks fish will give him a serpent" (Luke 11:11). In addition to biblical expectations of the father, there are clear legal obligations of the father. In general, these codes specify a responsibility for the economic welfare of the child; these obligations include food, clothing, and shelter. Fortunately, there are child support laws designed to enforce fulfillment of these fatherly obligations to his family. Lastly, the righteous father must assume the role of spiritual leader in the family. Probably, many of you have seen religious displays such as "The family that prays together, stays together" and "Bless this house, dear Lord, we pray." Beloved, such words are enchanting, but they require action patterns beyond mere reading. In this regard, the righteous father must emphasize the value of prayer, insist on grace before meals, encourage children to learn Bible verses, carry children to Sunday school, and remain with them during the worship period.

Additionally, the righteous father must talk with the children about original sin, the forgiveness made possible by Jesus, and the need for them to accept Jesus as Lord and Savior. In closing, the question may well become how righteousness is acquired. Isaiah the prophet reminds us that it comes not from within because our righteousness is but a filthy rag (Isa. 64: 6). Let us not become despondent, however, because God has already made provision for us to attain righteousness; is found in Romans 8:3, 5 and 10. Amen.

Chapter 6

The Biased Father

> Now Israel loved Joseph more than all his children because he was the son of his old age and he made a coat of many colors
>
> —Gen. 37:3

Father's Day is the third of four annually observe family worship Sundays. It is designed to pay tribute to the father for his efficient, dedicated, and ongoing services to and for the family. The concept *father* is associated with courage, protection, provisions, and leadership. Indications of this father model are reflected in such father-anchored statements as Adam, the father of humankind; Abraham, the father of the faithful; Lucifer, the father of lies, and God, the father of Jesus.

While there are other ways to view the word *father*, the sermon today will focus on a man who has fathered at least one child; however, the focal point is on how the father treats his children. Of particular in this sermon is the situation in which the father fails to treat his children equally. The sermon, in this connection, has been entitled "The Biased Father." It will examine three aspects of biased father, namely: biblical teaching on fatherhood, consequences of the biased father, and challenges for the contemporary father.

Although the position of father is historic, it has included many various functions at different time periods. During early civilization, the father was hunter, fisherman and defender of his family. Since that time, the father role who has undergone and expansion in types and obligations. In Colonial America, the father was conqueror of the wilderness, provider, and protector for his family. Since that time, the father role has become more diversified; it has included builder, employer, defender, and provider. In this twenty-first century, the father role is undergoing stress and strains caused largely by the economic downturn; hence, it is not unusual to find the father, unemployed, seeking even part-time work, and often in line for humanitarian distributions. Despite the mounting pressures on the father, he is nonetheless viewed as leader in his family within both the religious and social settings.

Against this synopsis on the role of father, attention will now be focused on the earlier specified dimensions of this sermon on the biased father. As used herein, the expression *biased father* denotes a father who shows inequities among his children with respect to praise, gifts, and other methods of commendation. With this definition of the biased father, the emphasis will now be directed to the first aspect of the sermon, which is biblical teachings on the role of father. Of the many scriptures on the father's responsibility to his family, only three will be used in this sermon. Each of the citation addresses a specific paternal obligation. The first is that of training. The Bible, in this connection calls upon the father to "train up the child in the way he should go and when he is old, he will not depart from it" (Pr.22:.6). Through this training process, the child becomes socialized and, therefore, acquires morals, values, respect, and a sense of responsibility to self and others. Since the body requires nutrients for normal growth and development, the Bible reminds the father of his responsibility to provide food for the child. Jesus was aware of this crucial need, and he, therefore, asked, "Or what man is there of you, who, if his son shall ask him for a loaf, will give him a stone?" (Matthew 7:9). Beloved, the nature of this question points to the father's responsibility to be an economic provider for his family. In Economics 201, it is taught that the economic function includes food, clothing, and shelter. Accordingly, the father should be committed to making provisions for all three of these needs. The third and final fatherly responsibility herein is the area of human relation, specifically the father-and-child relationship. In his letter of Ephesians, Saint Paul gave instruction to the father for his relationship. Thus, he wrote, "And ye fathers, provoke not your children to wrath, but bring them up in the nurture and admonition of the Lord" (Eph.6:4). Beloved, this verse clearly shows the father's obligation to spend quality time with his children, and in doing so, there will follow family unity and religious awareness. Unfortunately, there are innumerable instances in which family unity is married by parental inequities among the children.

This reality leads to the second aspect of the sermon, which is consequences of the biased father. The textual base of this sermon tells of an Old Testament personality who was a biased father. His name was Israel, originally known as Jacob. He was father of twelve sons, but he loved Joseph—a son born in his old age—more than the other sons. Israel gave Joseph a coat of many colors, and that act caused the brothers to be hostile toward Joseph. Later they conspired to rid themselves of Joseph by overpowering him and throwing him in a pit. Afterward, they took his coat, soaked it in blood, carried it back to their father, and reported that Joseph had been killed by an animal. Obviously, Israel was grieved and must have thought of how his earlier action toward Joseph had led to that sad ending. The ultimate outcome of that event had a happy ending; however, the emphasis today is to discourage the father from being biased in interacting with his children. This admonition leads to the final aspect of the sermon, which are challenges for the contemporary father.

In discussing this aspect of the sermon, attention is merely called the earlier examine factors involving the father. Hence the pertinent points will be cited herein. First, the father should avoid being biased in his relationships with the children. Next the father should be involved in the training of the children, especially in the area of religion. Thirdly, the father should strive to provide food, clothing, and shelter for the children, and finally, the father should avoid antagonizing, humiliating and threatening the children. When these guidelines are followed, the children will be happy, the father will be functioning in accordance with biblical teaching, and the Lord will be pleased with the father's stewardship. Happy Father's Day.

Chapter 7

The Grieving Yet Praying Father

> Take now thou, thine only son Isaac…and offer him there for a burnt offering upon one of the mountains while I will tell thee of.
>
> —Gen. 22:2

Today is the third annually observed family-focused worship service. It is known as Father's Day. This occasion engenders less sentimentality, fewer cards, a gift or two instead of flowers, less commercial advertising than is the activities for Mother's Day. The sermon of this 2015 Father's Day has been entitled "The Grieving Yet Believing Father." It will include the following three considerations, namely: the traditional father image, the grieving father, and the grieving and believing father.

Since the word *grieving* is a component of the subject, it is deemed appropriate to briefly elaborate on grieving. This word denotes the act of experiencing a lingering psychological feeling of hurt, loneliness, regret caused by illness, accident, death, or lingering worry about personal life experiences. Grieving is generally caused by or associated with losses, especially those caused by death. Clinical and pastoral counselors report of a type of grieving known as anticipatory grieving, which describes a situation in which a person, knowing the terminal condition of another, commences to experience emotions as if the individual had already expired. The media sources are becoming increasingly saturated of providing coverage of another type of grieving, known as cooperate grieving; the most recent setting at the writing of this sermon is the church shooting in Charleston, SC.

As with life in general, grieving, although highly emotional and energy draining—must be injured, and those grieving individuals will need to seek to mend the broken vessels in their life. The urgency of this need leads to the earlier specified components of this sermon, the first of which is the father image. As a prelude to analyzing the father image, a few observations on some types of fathers are herein submitted. There is God, the Heavenly Father, who is superior to all other fathers. On the religious strata, there is Pope Francis, the Holy Father of Catholicism. After Pentecost, the Apostles were known as Apostolic Fathers, and during the second through the fourth centuries, the religious leaders were known as the Church Fathers. Within the nonreligious arena, there were designation of fathers that included the father of our country, there was the head of the mafia known as the godfather, and there is the godfather who assumes some responsibility in helping with the responsibilities in rearing a child. Against this synopsis of selective father types, attention will now be directed to the first concern of the sermon, which is the father image.

The word *father* brings to mind a masculine individual who has procreated himself. He is viewed as being a masculine individual, robust, brave, and protective. He is a provider, defender, arbitrator, and highly visible in the family. The father, further, provides motivation, direction and encouragement for the family. When needed, the father administers discipline within biblical and legal guidelines. Finally, the father is the religious leader for the family. This overview on father leads to the next aspect, which is the grieving father. While the father is expected to be stoic and steadfast, he is nonetheless a human being with biological, psychological, and psycho-social characteristics. It, therefore, follows that the father may be trapped in the dilemma between the stoic giant and the emotional human being. Within such a situation, the father has experiences that engenders grief but is expected to conceal his hurts. While this paradox is not specifically labeled as such in the Bible, there are grief-producing experiences of fathers therein included. The first father, Adam, experienced a grief-producing situation when his son Cain killed Abel, his brother. Yet there is no record of Adam's grieving. In contrast, there is the account of David grieving over the death of his son Absalom who had earlier sought to kill him. How emotionally touching are David's words of grief— "The king [David] cried with a loud voice, O my son Absalom, O Absalom, my son, my son" (2nd Sam.19:4).

Between Adam and David was a father who was given a divine order that would cause grief, and yet, he made plans to carry out the responsibility. That biblical narrative will be the third and final point of the sermon; it is the grieving and yet believing father. Beloved, this emotionally draining narrative focuses on Abraham's order from God. It is found in Genesis 22:1-14 and, in this sermon is submitted for both individual and family reading. As brief background, God ordered Abraham to "get thee out of thy country, and from thy kindred, and from thy father's house, unto a land that I will shew thee." He complied, had a series of widely different experiences, receive two covenants from God, and sought to always comply with directives from God. Much to his dismay, Abraham received an order from God to offer his son, Isaac, as a sacrifice on a mountain that he would designate. To fulfill this divine order would cause a host of consequences that included killing, grief, loneliness—to mention but a few of the outcomes. Yet as the Bible notes, "Abraham believed God," so he commenced planning to carry out his assignment. He arose early, got Isaac up, they collected and packed the required equipment, and headed to the mountain. In the meantime, Abraham was doubtlessly experiencing a condition known as anticipatory grief—i.e., mentally, imagining how one will feel after the death of a person before the actual death occurs. This mental set was further intensified when Isaac inquired, "But where is the alarm for the burnt offering?" While grieving yet believing Abraham said unto Isaac, "My Son, God will provide himself a lamb for the burnt offering." Following that statement of both faith and assurance, the two of them went to the place where God had ordered, commenced to build the altar, bound and laid Isaac on the altar, and "took out a knife to slay his son." The narrative continues thus, "And the angel of the Lord called unto him out of heaven and said, Abraham, Abraham: and he said, 'Here Am I.' And he said, 'Lay not thine him upon the lad'…and Abraham looked, and behold…a ram caught in the thicket by his horns…and Abraham offered the ram as the sacrifice."

Beloved, this biblical narrative has contemporary implications for the whole of Christendom. Admittedly, the human sojourn is and encounters with mean-spirited people. Our responses, I feel, are to be prayerful, have courage, and even in disappointment like Abraham, grieve and yet believe that God has a ram in the thicket for your relief. Amen! Happy Father's Day 2015.

Chapter 8

Father Knows Best

And he said, a certain man had two sons: And the younger of them said his father, Father give me the portion of goods that falleth to me. And he divided unto them his living.

There was a sitcom on radio and television that ran from 1954—1960 entitled *Father Knows Best*. It was a comedy series that portrayed a middle-class family life in the Midwest. The father, played by Robert Montgomery, was a gentle, yet positive figure who knew and respected his position as head of the household. He was held by both his wife and children in high esteem. While allowing for self-expressions, the father always rendered decisions that showed that father knows best. Although it has been fifty-four years since that comedy ended, it's title still has relevance for contemporary times.

Even before the advent of that series, there existed a forerunner of that reality as reflected in the biblical account of the prodigal son. That account, as recorded by the gospel writer, Luke, will anchor our Father's Day 2014 sermon entitled "Father Knows Best." It will encompass the following three considerations, namely: the twenty- first-century father, the risk in prematurely leaving home, and the Heavenly Father's oversight and provisions It is an unfortunate fact that the title father has undergone innumerable changes in both form and function since the time of Adam, the federate head of the human family. These contemporary forms vary among nations as well as within nations. Of particular interest for this sermon is fatherhood in the United States of America. Accordingly, the focus will now be directed the first concern, which is the twenty-first-century Father. A casual glance and mere lay knowledge of America will immediately reveal an array of father types in this country. The most obvious demographic factor is that of race. In early colonial times, there was one group of white colonists. Those individuals were united in the common struggle for survival in the new land. While each family member was responsible for its chores along with some time for a group-planned community endeavors, it was the father who provided leadership in the family setting. He was the patriarch, protector, planner, and defender of the family plot. The father was also disciplinarian, a task he discharged with vigor and "the rod."

That a father-focused family continued after the advent of slavery, but it was nonexistent, except in rare instances, in the slave population. In fact, the general slave modality was to discourage marriage within the slave population. In those rare exceptions, the slave owner performed the marriage by having the couple jump over a broom-stick, and he pronounced them as being married. The general pattern, however, was no marriage in the slave population. It was within that inhumane setting where the quasi-family arose who was known as the black matriarch, a term coined by the late E. Franklin Frazier. That family structure prevailed throughout slavery, but it commenced to decline after Emancipation. There emerged respect for an increase in marriages among the emancipated people. The father, like his white counterpart, functioned as head of the household; he was decision maker, economic provider, and religious leader of his family. Unfortunately, that traditional family has undergone stress, strain, and radical change since the late '70s and becoming more visible in this twenty-first-century. Factors contributing to this disturbing reality include widespread drug participation, unemployment, incarceration, and the deliberate choice of black females to become mothers without a marital relationship with the child's father.

Beloved, this reality is on the rise. Children are being reared without a father and many by the child's grandparent rather than the mother. The resulting question becomes how can the father know best when he is unknown, in prison, in the drug culture, and unemployed? While this sad commentary is factual, it must not be forgotten that the larger society is the culprit in this matrix. It utilizes the black men in the underground economy, it renders difficult for even qualified black men to find employment, it issues lengthy prison terms for this group, and it seldom purges records of the offender. Hence, fatherhood in this black population is a precarious undertaking, and those men who take it seriously must heed the scriptural assertion, "looking unto Jesus who is the author and finisher of their faith."

The second concern of this sermon is that of prematurely leaving home. Numerous are the statistics on young people making a decision to leave home before they explore both the pros and cons of the decision. While many of them may have no father present, there is an inordinate number where the father is present. But like the prodigal son, the resources were soon depleted and his associates herein submitted—hopefully. There is no place like home, and if a father is present, remember father knows best. So, exercise, patience, prayer, thoughts on what if things don't work out before leaving home.

This admonition leads to the second consideration in the sermon—the risk in leaving home too soon. As noted in the textual anchor, that was a youngster who thought he knew—rather than his father—what was best for him. He is known as the prodigal son. Instead of expressing admiration for his father's love and economic provisions, he approached and said unto his father, "Give me the portion of goods that fall to me." The father asked no questions nor offered any warnings; instead, he complied with the son's request. The inexperienced son became engrossed in riotous living, and soon, his resources were depleted, his associates departed, his food needs were intensified, he sought employment in exchange for food, he was offered work feeding the pigs, he noted the pigs' consumption of husk, he was tempted to eat of the husk but came to himself, he thought, *how many hired servants of his father have bread enough to spare and I perish with hunger?* and he came to himself. He made three resolutions. I will arise, I will go, and I will say. That he did, and much to his surprise, his father saw him from far off. The prodigal was embraced and restored by his father.

Beloved, that glorious ending leads to the final dimension of this sermon, which is the Heavenly Father's oversight and concern for his followers. There is a song that asserts, "We are the Heavenly Father's children and he loves us one and all." This glorious affirmation does not prevent humankind from grievous actions nor adversities. Numerous are ungodly behaviors displayed by segments of humanity. Among these actions are assault, robbery, murder, drugs, prostitution, and home invasion. While these and many other problems are widespread, there is another category of problems that fall into the lives of believing Christian people. These problems include prolonged illness, loss of job, loss of home, disobedient children, dishonest spouse, loss of a spouse, and age-related problems. Beloved, the believer in a righteous God can so easily wonder where is the father who knows the best. To such troubled persons, the good news, is that the father knows just how much can you bear. Further, there are two biblical teachings that must be read and believed; one is Job of the Old Testament and the other, Peter, of the New Testament. The episode of Job is cited because he was a righteous, prosperous, a family man, and believe in God. Yet adversities befell him, and he suffered immensely. Believing that the father knows best, Job uttered, "Of all my appointed days. I will wait until my change comes," and in another context, "When he try me, I shall come forth as pure gold." Peter, in commenting on the suffering wrote, "But the God of all grace who has called us into his eternal glory by Christ Jesus, after that ye have suffered a while, make you perfect, established, strengthen, settle you." (1st Peter 5:10).

So, in closing this 2014 Father's Day sermon, let us pray to live one day at a time, and despite our disappointments, remember that God the father knows best. Amen. Happy Father's Day.

Chapter 9

The Dilemma of Motherhood

> And she was in bitterness of soul, and prayed unto the lord and wept so.
>
> —1st Samuel 1:10–11

The history of Mother's Day can be traced back to a Sunday school teacher whose name was Anna Jarvis. She felt that mothers, the bulwark of society, were accorded little value other than as laborers. Their task seemed endless; their energies seemed inexhaustible, their accomplishments seemed elusive, their families seemed unappreciative, and their dreams seemed nebulous. Yet the mothers, according to Ms. Jarvis, continued their commitment to the family. Thus, she reasoned a time should be set aside to give homage to the backbone of the family, and she, therefore, proposed a Sunday to be designated as Mother's Day. The idea fell on fertile soul; it later received a presidential proclamation that designated the second Sunday in May as Mother's Day. Since that time, there have been Sundays designated for family members that include Youth Day, Father's Day, and Grandparent's Day.

Mother's Day stands alone as the most recognized and seemingly cherished family observation day. Our sermon, in keeping with this national emphasis, will be focused on mothers, and has been entitled "The Dilemma of Motherhood." It will explore the role of motherhood in three different historical periods, namely: Old Testament history, Colonial America, and contemporary America with emphasis on the African-American family.

Prior to an analysis of these periods, attention will be focused first on the word *dilemma* or a baffling situation in which a person is torn between at least two competing choices with equal appeal. One poet has described it in the words, "To be or not to be." In the production *A Raisin in the Sun*, the widowed grandmother faced a dilemma in deciding how to disperse insurance funds from the death of her husband between the medical aspiration of the daughter and the business venture of the son. Within the slightly different context, the prolific New Testament writer St. Paul faced a dilemma as reflected in his statement, "For the good that I would I do not: But the evil which I would not that I do" (Romans 7:19). In sum, a dilemma is a setting, in which a person is torn between two choices.

While dilemmas are widespread in daily life, they tend to be more frequent and energy-draining in motherhood. A glance at biblical history shows the existence of a dilemma in the first family of Adam and Eve. Even before she became a mother, Eve faced the dilemma of choosing between the mandate of God and the temptation of Satan (Genesis 1:4-5).

From this brief discussion of the word *dilemma* attention will now be directed to the first of three concerns in the sermon; it is that of the family during Old Testament history. The first biblical family consisted of Adam, Eve, Cain, Abel, and later Seth. By type, it was known as monogamous or one husband and one wife. In later Old Testament history, however, there were instances in which one man had several wives. Generally, those unions are given a low profile in America in an effort to highlight the traditional biblical model of one husband and one wife. The fact is, however, that some prominent Old Testament men had several wives; among such men were Abraham who used Hagar for sexual purposes, Jacob who had two wives and two female servants, Elkanah who had two wives, and King Solomon who had a hundred wives.

The textual basis of this Mother's Day sermon was lifted from the account of Elkanah. One of his wives was barren; her name was Hannah, while the other Peninnah was productive. Hannah was troubled by her barrenness notwithstanding the fact that Elkanah would give more of his possessions to her than to Peninnah. But Hannah was distraught. Worldly goods meant less than a child to her. She loved her husband, she knew the custom of her time in which a man could have more than one wife, and she felt that her husband might secretly care more for the woman who was the mother of his child. In this context, Hannah had a dilemma. She was literally at the crossroad. She was torn between two choices, and she was distraught by thoughts of the incorrect choice. In an effort to solve her dilemma, Hannah decided to take her burden to the Lord. Accordingly, she went with her husband and Peninnah up to the temple of worship. There she secretly slipped away from the group and approached the mercy seat. Friends, as the text speaks to us today, we learned that Hannah, although in bitterness, prayed unto the Lord (v.10) in which she asked to be made fertile and promised to give her child into service for the Lord (11). Here again, is a dilemma—give me a child and I will give the child to you. This prayer acknowledge that she was childless, but it also conveyed her fervent desire to have a child. The Bible says that the Lord listened and granted her request. In return, Hannah fulfilled her vow, and the rest is Old Testament history. Her child was the name Samuel who later became a priest, and he authored two books of the Old Testament, the 1st and 2nd Samuel.

Having looked at the family in Old Testament history, let us now turn to the second topic—motherhood in America. Family sociologists agree that two distinct types of motherhood prevail in America. These types are labeled as Eurocentric and Afrocentric. The first refers to the European, or white, type of motherhood while the second, Afrocentric, is used to designate the black family in America. There are obvious differences in the expectations and privileges of these types. In the Eurocentric setting, the mother has the option of housekeeper, mother, and woman of leisure while in the later setting, the mother must combine motherhood with work, often the sole gainfully employed member of the household.

Another difference is seen in the prominence given to white mothers in contrast to exploitation imposed on black mothers. Continuing the differences, most white mothers pick up their children after school whereas black mothers arrange for their children to remain in the post-school or after-care program. Although this difference is troublesome, it was even worse during slavery—a fact echoed in an utterance by Sojourner Truth in which she exclaimed, "I had many chullen but the greatest hurt for me was to have my baby snatched from my arms an took away, but body knows the hurt, but King Jesus and me. Friends, many years separate us today from the time of slavery, but a more sinister and destructive force is eroding black motherhood.

This somber fact leads to the final topic, namely contemporary African-American motherhood. In Staples' book on the black family, this situation is labeled as the death of black motherhood. This contemporary scene is marred by the drug culture, prostitution, same-sex unions, pornography, and "live in" arrangements. Ironically, white society benefits from this lifestyle, situation known as black pathology. This expression denotes problems in the black society, but capitalism and profits from it. Through a continuance of babies, doctors and other health care providers have patients, insurance companies pay claims, and mother get benefits. The black men in the meantime keeps public defenders in business, jails filled, food vendors afloat, and employment beyond the reach of those with criminal records.

Friends, the times are critical and the cloud of impending neo slavery is become darker. The offset such a disastrous fate, we black Americans must institute a concerted effort to instill religious values in our children. We must support our mothers, we must discipline our children, we must monitor the school system, we must pray together, we must worship together, we must work together, and we must reinforce the worth of each other. Beloved when we attain this level of unity, our children will reflect the values extolled in two different poems that will close our sermon on the dilemma of motherhood. One is "The Village Blacksmith" by Longfellow.

> He goes on Sunday to the church.
> He sits among his boys;
> He hears the Parson pray and preach.
> He hears his daughter's voice,
> Singing in the village choir,
> ....
> It sounds to him like his mother's voice,

How in the grave she lies and with his strong
brawny hand he wipes away a tear from his eyes.
Lastly, Kipling's "Mother o' Mine."
I was damned of body and soul,
I know whose voice would make me whole,
Mother o' mine, O mother o' mine!

In closing, both of these poetic depictions of motherhood are enchanting, emotional and endearing, but they fall short of summarizing the ultimate test of motherhood, despite her dilemma, as in Proverbs, "Her children arise up and call her blessed, her husband also, and he praiseth her (v.28). May God bless all here assembled, and to all mother, our membership joins me in extending best wishes for a glorious Mother's Day in the year of our Lord, 2008.

Chapter 10

The Praying Mother

> O Lord of host, if thy will indeed look on the affliction of thy handmaid.
>
> —1ˢᵗ Samuel 1:11

There are four family-oriented Sundays each calendar year, they are, in the order of occurrence, Mother's Day, Youth Day, Father's Day, and Grandparents' Day. Each of these days engenders, sentimental feelings, but Mother's Day stands alone as the most emotionally saturated family observation. It is also the day of greatest church attendance in commemorating these four family-focused Sundays. In addition to, if not before, family worship are numerous other activities; the giving of cards, flowers, phone calls, visiting, and dining out. In the language of a pioneer television program *Queen for a Day,* Mother's Day provides an opportunity for a mother to experience the excitement of being queen for a day.

While expressions of gratitude are certainly appropriate for Ms. Anna Jarvis whose persistent efforts led to the establishment of Mother's Day it must be remembered that there were prominent mothers during early biblical history. One of those mothers was Hannah whose experiences are recorded in the 1ˢᵗ Samuel chapters 1 and 2.

Hannah first appears on the scene as one of Elkanah's two wives; unlike the other wife who had children, Hannah was barren. Since she greatly desired children; Hannah was heavily laden. Rather than to accept her destiny, Hannah chose to pray about the problem. From that decision and her firm belief in prayer, Hannah would later become a mother and, at the same time, emerge as a praying mother.

Knowing that mothers of today have various needs, decisions, and aspirations, our 2010 Mother's Day sermon has been entitled "The Praying Mother". It will be anchored by the following three dimensions, namely: praying for self, praying for a blessing, and keeping the promise uttered in prayer. As background for the sermon, attention is called to its textual base, which is the first chapter of Samuel. Therein is the account of a man Elkanah, who—

according to the customs of the time—had two wives. He was a religious man and cared for his wives and the children. Much to the anguish of one wife, Hannah no child had been born to her at the opening of this narrative. Her husband nonetheless loved her, but Hannah felt dejected. In keeping with the family custom, Hannah joined Elkanah and Peninnah as they journey to Shiloh for worship.

After the religious ceremony, it seems that Hannah slipped away from the family to pray; she was in bitterness of soul and felt compelled to pray, and that she did.

This brief account leads to the earlier specified dimensions of the subject, the first one is praying for self. As earlier noted, Hannah was barren and greatly desired to become a mother. It is of interest to note that no record exists to show that she was hostile toward her husband nor belligerent toward Peninnah or even the children. Instead, Hannah viewed her situation as being between the Lord and herself, a fact she would express to Eli, the priest. Owing to her mixture of bitterness and grief, Hannah appeared to be intoxicated as she sought to pray. Eli, upon seeing her, inquired as to how long she had been drinking. Hannah told him that she did not drink but was a woman of grief and had come to pour out her anguish to the Lord. Sensing her sincerity, Eli instructed her to go in peace, and the God of Israel would grant her petition.

Beloved, in the process of time, God granted Hannah's desire. This scriptural teaching leaps across the annals of time and speaks to mother and those who desire to become mothers; the message is loud and clear. Avoid anger, jealousy, and destructive thoughts for they block the pathway to God's storehouse of blessings. Instead, seek to become a praying woman or mother because great are the demands of motherhood.

This somber admonition leads to the second concern in the sermon, which is the prayer called petition. As noted in verses 17 and 18, Hannah uttered a prayer of petition. Remember, she had earlier prayed about her barrenness, but now she goes to another level. Her focus is elevated to utter a request for a male child with a promise that she would give him to the Lord (11). Unlike the other wife, Hannah was willing to offer her son, if granted, to the Lord. This generous act certainly was not to please her husband; instead, it was a sacrifice to show appreciation for her gift from God. Additionally, she was grateful for the shift in her femininity from barrenness to fertility. This behavior was another indication of the praying mother. As history would soon demonstrate, Hannah's sacrifice would become a shining star in the history of Israel. The question, in this connection, becomes what type of child are mothers of the day sending into the world?

This question leads to the final aspect of this sermon on the praying mother, which is keeping the promise. Hannah's action after the birth of Samuel epitomizes the act of keeping a promise made to God. While this level of promise keeping is the highest form, it must be remembered that any ethical, prayerful, and sincere promise should be fulfilled by the one who made it. It is unfortunate, however that the general human response is to beseech and frequently after which little, if any, efforts are made to fulfill the earlier divine petition or human promise. The life of Hannah, in this connection, sends a lucid message to humanity, especially Christian believers, to think before making a promise, to be cognizant when time comes to comply with it, and to be grateful of the opportunity to have earlier realized its actuality. Imagined for a moment, how happy Hannah must have been to become a mother, how she craved to keep the child, how lonely she might have been without the child residing with her, but she remembered and keep her promise. Certainly, she rejoiced in having her barrenness removed in having a male child and fulfilling her promise to give the child to the Lord's service. Oh, mother think for a moment on the magnitude of Hannah's gift! That little boy would one day be called by God; he would later become a prophet, an intercessor, a priest, and a judge. What an illustration list of accomplishments by a young lad who was given to service for the Lord.

In closing, hopefully our fellowship in specific and motherhood in general, are committed to giving to the world not only the boys but girls as well who will make a significant contribution for the welfare of humanity and the glory of God. Our continual prayer for mothers, especially, today is that they will remember the three points of this sermon, which are in distress pray to the Lord instead of blaming others, to be specific in your prayer request, and to deliver on the petition once it has been granted.

Remember, God is counting on you, and your child may well have the confidence in your prayer as noted in the words of Kipling,

> If I were hanged on the highest hill
> ....
> I know whose love would follow me still
> Mother o' mine, O mother o' mine.
> ....
> If I were damned of both body and soul
> I know whose prayers would make me whole.
> Mother o' mine, O mother o' mine.
>
> May the God of Grace and Glory, bless and keep our mothers. Amen.

Chapter 11

The Prevailing Mother

> Have mercy on me, O Lord, thou Son of David, my daughter is grievously vexed with the devil.
>
> —Mt. 15:22

Today is the most emotionally charged day of the year. Thanks to Ms. Anna Jarvis, it is known as Mother's Day and has national recognition. Although its origin was to tender tribute to mother for her tender, love, care and provisions, Mother's Day is now engulfed by commercial interest. Admittedly, the roses, cards, calls, gifts, and dinner outing all create an ecstasy for the mother; however, those experiences are short in duration, ranging from a single day to a weekend. In the meantime, studies of motherhood have shown that the mother craves more for day-to-day appreciation and love rather than a single day or weekend of overwhelming expressions of gratitude. Although the mother is thought of as being compassionate, understanding, and encouraging, she must nonetheless function in an increasingly competitive, impersonal, and exploitative society. She must, therefore, assume proactive stance and, thereby, utilize the fine art of confrontation or literally bite the bullet.

Our 2008 Mother's Day sermon will address this need using as a subject the prevailing mother. The sermon will be anchored by the following three dimensions, namely: systematic problem areas for the mother, a role model for the mother, and outcomes for the prevailing mother. Prior to analyzing these concerns, attention will be focused on two words: *systemic* and *prevail*. The first word, *systemic,* refers to components of society that include the economy, the social system, the judicial system, the religious system, the family setting and the neighborhood. The second concept, *prevail,* as used today denotes the ability to be strong, resilient, steadfast, persuasive, determined and courageous.

Having defined these two terms, attention will now be directed to the easier specified concerns—the first of which is systemic problem areas for the mother. Beloved, the areas are numerous, complex, and often have unpredictable consequences. Accordingly, this sermon will be confined to three of the problem areas; they are the family, the school, and the church. In this order they shall be analyzed with the family being first.

Students of the social sciences concur that the family is the most significant unit in society. It is an unfortunate fact that this unit is undergoing stress and strain; further, its foundation is under assault by sinister forces that include promiscuity, the drug culture, unemployment, gang violence, and school dropouts. The one gleam of hope for survival is that of having a prevailing mother within the household. It is the mother who functions as the backbone of the family. She is the source of nurture, food preparation, motivation, goal setting, consolation, and often supplemental—if not the only source of—income. Complicating this plethora of problems is the presence of a non-supportive husband or a live-in.

The second area in which the mother must prevail is that of the school system. It is she who provides the initial learning experiences for the child. She is, also the one who must monitor the child's performance, attend the PTO meetings and school related-activities, and pick up the child from the extended-day program. In fulfilling these and numerous other chores, the mother must remain committed to the task of motherhood. Oh! There will be times when the family demands will cause the mother poetically to shutter and grow sick at heart, but in those distressful moments, she should embrace the biblical teaching," I can do all things through Christ which strengthen me" (Phil. 4:13).

The third area in which the mother must prevail is that of religion (Christianity for us here gathered today). It is the mother who is usually the one to introduce the child to morals, ethics, and a faith orientation. She is the one who will introduce the child to the nursery prayer, "Now lay me down to sleep." She is the one who will read biblical stories to the child; she is the one who will dress the child for worship service and, often, drive the child to the place of worship. In view of these religious dimensions of the mother who prevails, it should come as no surprise to find that children tend to embrace the faith anchor of their mother with the lone exception being those in religiously mixed marriage, especially, with the Protestant mother and the Catholic father.

Having examined three system areas, attention will now be directed to the second concern, which is that of a role model for the mother who prevails. Numerous are the types of and sources for a role model. However, there is one that stands alone in effectiveness. It is found in the Holy Bible and described in a book entitled *All the Women of the Bible* by Ruth Reed. She is described by Reed as "a mother who had suffered unbearable tribulation because of the affliction of her daughter who was grievously vexed with a devil" (Mt. 15:22). She was viewed as an outsider by nationality, language, and religion. Despite those barriers, that mother sought Jesus with the whom she prevails on behalf of her child. The persistence of this Syro-Phoenician woman yielded a positive outcome, and therefore, provides insights on being a prevailing mother. For a few moments, let us look at this Syro-Phoenician woman to gleam insights on how to be a prevailing mother. Read describes her as having heard about Jesus and his works. She knew that Jesus could solve her problem, she walked toward Jesus with courage and faith, and she presented her case by saying unto Jesus, "Have mercy on me, O Lord, thou Son of David, my daughter is grievously vexed with the devil" (Mt.15:22).

Strange though it was, Jesus ordered that she be sent away. She nonetheless continued to prevail because Jesus said unto her, "I am not sent but unto the lost sheep of the house of Israel" (Mt.15:24).

The woman heard him, but she continued to prevail by saying, "Lord, help me" (Mt. 15: 54). In response, Jesus said, "It is not meet to take the children's bread and cast it to dogs" (Mt. 25: 26). Many timid women would have given up by this time, but not that mother! Instead, she said, "Truth let the dogs eat of the crumbs which fall from their masters' table" (Mt. 15: 27). At last, her unshakable faith was ready to yield a reward for persistency. Hence, Jesus said, "O woman, great is thy faith" (Mt.15: 28). And from that moment, her daughter was made whole."

Beloved, this account of the Syro-Phoenician woman leaps across the annals of time and beacons to all mothers with a prevail, especially with the Triune God. This glorious challenge leads to the final consideration in this sermon on the prevailing mother; it is that all of the outcomes for the mother who prevails. Instead of an extensive review of studies on motherhood, attention will be confined just to two sources; one is the Bible and the other is literature. The citations will be lifted with comment. First, the biblical outcomes are the following. "Train up a child in the way he should go: And when he is old, he will not depart from it (Prov. 22:6) and "Her children arise up and call her blessed; her husband, also, and he praiseth her" (Proverbs 31: 28).

Next, "The Village Blacksmith" by Longfellow signals a poignant outcome as reflected in the words.

> He goes on Sunday to the Church,
> He hears the parson pray and preach
> He hears his daughter's voice singing in the Village choir,
> ....
> It sounds to like his mother's voice,
> How in the grave she lies, and with his strong
> brawny hand, he wipes a tear from his eyes.

This seems to concur with Kipling's "Mother o' Mine"
Best wishes for mothers in 2009. Amen.

Chapter 12

The Overzealous Mother

Lord, allow one of my sons to sit on the right

—Matt. 20:20–23

Today is the most emotionally charge day of the year. Thanks to Ms. Anna Jarvis, it is now known as Mother's Day and has national recognition. Although its origin was the pay tribute to mothers for their tender love and care, Mother's Day is now engulfed by commercial interest. Admittedly, the roses, cards, calls, gifts and dinner outing all create ecstasy for the mother; however, those experiences are short in duration ranging from a single day to a weekend. Studies of motherhood have shown that the mother craves more for day-to-day appreciation, love and help than a weekend of overwhelming expressions of short-lived gratitude.

Although the mother is often viewed as the silent mover in the family situation, there are times when she can become overzealous in efforts to advance her children. While there are motherly desires for the child's welfare, they should be tempered with considerations of factors such as the child's temperament, capabilities, interest, and likelihood of success. This assertive tendency of the mother is no recent tendency; instead, it can be traced back to biblical times. Our sermonette today, entitled "The Overzealous Mother" will examine to aspects of this motherly ambition, namely: what are factors that and gender this overzealousness and how does the motherly desire fit into the child welfare? Although the scriptural anchor has been lifted from the New Testament where the account is found of a mother who wanted her sons to sit beside Jesus, there were earlier instances of mothers who were overzealous. This fact leads to the first consideration, which is *what are factors that cause a mother to be overzealous?* Responses to this question can be found in both the Bible and worldly books. The Bible, for example, contains no reference to Eve, the first mother, as being overzealous; but it soon shows Sarah, the wife of Abraham, as being overzealous following the birth of her son Isaac. Having earlier encouraged Abraham to father a child by her maidservant. Sarah, after the birth of Isaac, insisted that Abraham would remove Hagar and Ishmael for the household; her intent was to have Isaac reared in the household of his father and mother. Another example of the overzealous mother was Rebecca who deceived her husband by plotting to have Jacob receive Esau's blessings; her intent was to have Jacob become the blessed one even by trickery.

There are many other Old Testament mothers worthy of consideration, but the emphasis will now be focused on the textual mother. Remember, it is the account of the mother who wanted her two sons to sit beside Jesus, one on the right and the other on the left. Friends, in all of the mothers herein cited, not a single one communicated with a child about its desire; instead, they were more concerned about pursuing their own agendas. Admittedly, many years separate those biblical mothers from today, yet there is yet the tendency for some mothers to become overzealous about enhancing the destiny of their children. Beloved, it is not herein argued that mothers should remain aloof with respect to the child's welfare. Instead, it is submitted that the mother should be aware of the child's interest, capability, and likelihood of succeeding before moving too aggressively to thrust the child into a threatening situation. It is the fact that our society is too saturated with competitions, upward mobility, fame, and success while placing two little emphases on molding the child for entrance into the hostile environment. What are needed in parental interaction, monitoring, and assistance with homework—all in an effort to get to know the child. Admittedly, the process may seem long and, at times, useless, but the mother should remain focused but not overbearing.

This fact leads to the second and final aspect of the sermon; it is that of how the mother's desire fit into the life vision of the child. While there is much support for motherly concern in planning the child's future, care must be exercised in the purpose and methods used in the process. In the interest of time, attention will be called to two situations in which the mother was overzealous. The first had an adverse or negative consequence. It is the account of Rebecca whose overzealousness for her younger twin son Jacob connived with him to fool his father, Isaac, and steal Esau's blessing. Although friends in the long run, Jacob was deceived by his uncle, Laban, after having worked for seven years in order to marry Rebecca. This biblical account sends a message to mothers, which is not to stoop a trickery to promote your child's welfare because in the long run the child will suffer. The second example contains another biblical teaching about the zealousness of motherhood. It is the textual account where the mother of Zebedee's children with her sons were worshiping Jesus and desiring a certain thing of him. "And he said unto her, "What wilt Thou?' She said unto him, 'Grant that these my two sons may sit, the one of thy right hands, and the other on the left, in the kingdom.' But Jesus answered and said, Ye know not what ye asked? Are ye able to drink of the cup that I shall dream of, and to be baptized with the baptism that I am baptized with? They say unto him, "We are able...' 'It is the fathers to give."

In closing, mothers and all others who have child-rearing responsibilities, the sermon signals clearly that you must temper your zeal with prayer.

Chapter 13

The Sacrificing Mother

> O my Lord, give her the living child, and in no wise slay it. Then the king answered and said, give her the living child, and in no wise slay it; she is the mother thereof.
>
> —1st Kings 3:26–27

There are four family-oriented Sundays each calendar year; they are, in the order of occurrence, Mother's Day, Youth Day, Father's Day, and Grandparent's Day. Each of these days engenders sentimental feelings, but Mother's Day stand alone as the most emotionally saturated family observation. It is also the day of greatest church attendance in commemorating these four family focused Sundays. In addition to, if not before, family worship are numerous other activities; the giving of cards, flowers, phone calls, visiting, and dining out. In the language of the pioneer television program *Queen for a Day*, Mother's Day provides an opportunity for mother to experience the excitement of being queen for a day. While expression of gratitude is certainly appropriate for Ms. Anna Jarvis whose persistent efforts led to the establishment of Mother's Day; it must be remembered that their prominent mothers during early biblical history. Some of them were named: Eve, Sarah, and Hannah.

However, several were unnamed but highly visible in the arena of motherhood.

One of these unnamed mothers will anchor the sermon today, entitled "The Sacrificing Mother." The sermon will encompass four dimensions of the sacrificing mother, namely: synopsis of motherhood, major role expectations of the mother, motherhood in the African-American population, and the textual presentation on the sacrificing mother. Since the sermon is rooted in both biblical and contemporary history, the usual historical background will be omitted. Instead, the focus will be placed on the earlier specified concerns, the first which is a synopsis of motherhood.

Historically, this word has denoted a female who performs an array of functions for her child or children. Being the biological mother of the offspring is viewed as the beginning of a lengthy conglomerate of responsibilities and functions necessary for the child's welfare. As is known by mothers and often noted by fathers, motherhood encompasses seemingly never-ending duties, expectations, sacrifices, and even personal neglects. The obligations of motherhood can be likened unto the old adage "a father works from sun to sun, but a mother's work is never done." The position of motherhood is further complicated by its multiple role expectations, some of which are cooking, housekeeping, caring for all members of the household, coping with an overdemanding husbands or live-in associates, and even being employed outside. In this regard, motherhood is often an ongoing period of stress and strain. But fortunately, women throughout history have undertaken the task of motherhood. Thus, children, families, neighborhoods, schools, worship centers, and geographical areas all have experienced a positive impact from the presence of dedicated motherhood.

This fact leads to the second aspect of the sacrificial mother; it is role expectation of this mother type. It is a truism that motherhood encompasses just about everything that can be in envisioned. It starts with childbirth and rapidly expand to include nurturing, dressing, training, mentoring, disciplining, motivating, defining appropriate goals, preparation for school, instilling religious values, along with being the center of household activities, and maintaining peace and tranquility within the household.

The third focus of this sermon is directed to a special type of motherhood, which is that of motherhood in the African-American population. Friends, many years separate us today from the time of slavery, but a more sinister and destructive force is eroding black motherhood. This somber fact leads to the final topic—contemporary African- American motherhood. In Staples' book on the black family, this situation is labeled as the death of black motherhood. This contemporary scene is marred by the drug culture, prostitution, same-sex unions, pornography, and "live in" arrangement. Sadly, white society benefits from this lifestyle, a situation known as black pathology. This expression denotes problems in the black society, but capitalism profits from it. Through a continuance of babies, doctors, and other health care providers have patients, insurance companies pay claims, and employment beyond the reach of those with criminal records. Friends, the times are critical and the cloud of impending neo-slavery is become darker. To offset such a disastrous fate, we black Americans must institute a concerted effort to instill religious values in our children, we must support out mothers, we must discipline our children, we must worship together, we must work together, and we must reinforce the worth of each other. Beloved, when this level of unity has been attained, our children will reflect the values extolled in two different poems that will close our sermon on the dilemma of motherhood. One is the "Village Blacksmith" by Longfellow.

> He goes on Sunday to the Church,
> he sits among his boys,
> he hears the Parson pray and preach.
> He hears his daughter's singing in the village choir,
> ....
> it sounds to him like his mother's voice,
> how in the grave she lies and with his strong
> brawny hand he wipes away a tear from his eyes.

This somber poem leads to the final concern of the sermon which is the textual anchor that described a mother who had a great sacrifice in order for her child to live. The narrative of this sacrifice is found in 1st Kings 3:16-27. Briefly, two women that were harlots came to King

Solomon for him to decide which one was the child's mother. It seems that one of the women was accused of taking the baby at night from its blood mother. Obviously, the real mother protested against action. Hence, they found themselves in the presence of King Solomon whose decision they were obligated to accept. After much dialogue with vastly different opinions, the king called for a sword for the purpose of dividing the baby so each woman could have half of the child. The fake mother agreed, but the real mother cried aloud, "O my lord, give her the living child and in no wise slay it"—what a sacrifice giving up the child for its safety, to probably never see it again. But Solomon, the wise king, under divine inspiration determined the real mother and gave the child to her. Amen.

Chapter 14

The Altruistic Mother

> She vowed and said…(if thou will give unto me)…a male child then I will him unto the Lord.
>
> —1st Sam. 1:11

The Bible asserts that creation is the handiwork of God (Gen. 1, Ps. 19:1). It consisted of six days endeavor. The divine process included the making of man in his own image, who was to have dominion over the creation. In divine wisdom, God said, "It is not good that man should be alone; I will make him a help meet known as Eve." (Gen. 3:20 and 4:11). She became the first mother in biblical history when Cain was born. Although Eve was the first mother of humanity, the Bible identifies an array of mothers in both the Old and New Testament. The mothers had similarities, but they possessed great differences and even some unique nesses.

Our 2014 Mother's Day sermon will be anchored by the life of a mother who prayed to the Lord for a male child and promised to give him to the Lord (1st Sam. 1:11). The woman, Hannah, can be labeled as altruistic, a word that denotes giving of one's self for the welfare of another without anticipation of returns from the person(s) who benefitted from the earlier action. Although Jesus was the world's greatest altruist, Hannah's commitment to give her requested male child was clearly an indication of altruism. Accordingly, the sermon today will focus on Hannah as the altruistic mother. It will include three dimensions, namely: a profile of Hannah, impediments to motherhood, and the continuum of motherhood.

Since this sermon is deeply rooted in the history of an Old Testament personality, the traditional historical anchor will be omitted, and instead, the focus is directed to the earlier specified concerns—the first of which is a profile of Hannah. Whereas the word *profile* is defined as an outline or contour of the human face, especially the face viewed from one side, it will have a wider use in this sermon. Its parameters will include the overall person, including, genders, living arrangement, general behavior, and spirituality, if evidenced. Hence, profile as used herein with respect to Hannah encompasses the total person known as Hannah. She lived at a time when a man could have more than a wife. Hannah, therefore, had to share her husband, Elkanah, with his other wife, Peninnah, who was the mother of his children. Hannah, in meantime, was childless. At the time of the yearly sacrifice, Elkanah gave a portion to Peninnah and to her children. But he also gave a worthy portion to Hannah because he loved her notwithstanding the fact that the Lord had shut up her womb. Elkanah was aware of Hannah's grief, and he sought to console her by asking, "Am I not better to thee than ten sons" (1st Sam. 1:8). His attempt to quell Hannah's grief was to no avail because she refused to eat or drink at the feast with Eli the priest. Instead, Hannah went to the temple place for prayer. "And she was in bitterness of soul, and prayed unto the Lord, and wept sore," Hannah prayed in her heart; only her lips moved but her voice was not heard. Eli noted her unusual prayer modality and incorrectly concluded that she was intoxicated and, therefore, asked her how long she had been drunken. Hannah assured Eli that her action was not from being drunk; instead, it was an expression of a sorrowful spirit. Upon hearing her earnest desire and prayer to become a mother of male child, Eli instructed her to go in peace. "And the God of Israel grant thee thy petition that thou hast asked of him."

Taking a quantum leap forward, Hannah was blessed with a child who was given the name Samuel. True to her earlier commitment, Hannah carried the child to live with Eli the priest. Beloved, the rest is history, i.e., Samuel's leadership and impact on Israel's history. In the meantime, a backward glance shows Hannah as an altruistic mother; she pleaded with the Lord for a male child; she promised to give the child to service for the Lord; and Hannah fades into the annals of biblical history. In sum, her profiles epitomize the altruistic mother.

This heartwarming account of Hannah leads to the seconds concern of the sermon. Which are impediments to motherhood. This concern focuses on obstacles, problems, and alternatives that have an impact on motherhood. There are some biological obstacles to motherhood. Infertility or the inability to become impregnated is a recurring problem notwithstanding medical technology. It can be traced back to the time of Hannah, the person upon which the sermon is based. Barrenness was an obstacle even before Hannah; it plagued Sarah, the wife of Abraham. Owing to her initial inability to have a child, Sarah encouraged Abraham to—in biblical terms—go into her maidservant, Hagar. He did, and Hagar bore him a son who was named Ishmael. Many have been and continue to be a woman who are medically unable to have children.

The second difficulty in motherhood is that of socio-cultural problems. Included in this configuration is the inability to obtain gainful employment to adequately provide food, shelter, clothing, and reasonable activities for the child. In those infrequent work settings, often the hours are long, the pay is low, and the work schedule can so frequently render the mother little, if any, quality time with the children. Another facet of these cultural problems exists in an area known as black pathology. This expression encompasses activities such as the drug culture, prostitution, incarceration, child neglect, abuse, and even abandonment. Sadly, there is another increasing problem area for motherhood, and it is that of the working mother supporting the "pie back" male, not husband, who drives her to work and then uses the vehicle to visit other women. In contrast to this reality, there are women who desire to be married and rear a family. The problem, however, is the fact that there are so few eligible, employed, reputable men available. Therefore, many females choose rather to remain single or seek a significant other within a large demographic arena. In response to this problem, there is trend for females to use medical interventions and/or enter into a non-legally binding relationship to institute fertilization.

Despite the array of options and problems associated with motherhood, there are a host of dedicated women who are yet committed to the sacred task of motherhood. This glorious fact leads to the third, and last, dimension of this 2014 Mother's Day Sermon, which is the continuum of motherhood. The range is from altruism to egoism. Essentially, this range is submitted to briefly depict the styles in motherhood. As noted in the sermon title, *altruism* is the Undergirding word. This style of motherhood is one in which the mother subordinates her personal desires, plans, and achievements to actions, prayers, and resources to the provision, training, monitoring, praying, and overseeing the child's safety, development, and general welfare. In contrast, the egoistic mother places attention on herself first and then maybe directs some efforts to helping the child.

According to a prominent sociologist, there is an emerging pattern known as the death of motherhood by the biological mother, but thanks be to God there is the safety net known as the grandmother, a lady who undertakes the task of rearing another generation. In closing, it is my prayers and anticipation that our mothers here are of the altruistic rather than the egoistic types. Further, that their child or children can concur with Kipling's "Mother o' Mine."

> If I were hanged on the highest hill,
> Mother o' mine, O mother o' mine!
> I know whose love would follow me still,
> Mother o' mine, O mother of mine!
> If I were drowned in the deepest sea,
> Mother o' mine, O mother o' mine!
> I know whose tears would come down to me,
> Mother o' mine, O mother o' mine!
>
> If I were damned of body and soul,
> I know whose prayers would make me whole,
> Mother o' mine, O mother o' mine!

God Bless, and Happy Mother's Day.

Chapter 15

Knowing Your Whereabouts

> And Samuel said unto Jesse, Are here all thy children? And he said, there remaineth yet the youngest, and behold, he keepeth the sheep. And Samuel said unto Jesse, send and fetch him: For We will not sit down till he come hither.
>
> —1st Samuel 16:11

During the early history of America, there were few people, and they engaged in mutual activities for their personal welfare. Neighbors were concerned about the entire group, family members shared a common interest in survival, and every person was diligent about being at his/her place of assignment. That practice of being at one's station was of great value since a person could so easily get lost, be attacked by wild animals, or even killed by an Indian. Hence, to help in location should one misses, the colonists developed the custom of being in one's place; it was also known as knowing your whereabouts.

Many years separate out time from the colonial era, and numerous have been the changes; some positive but many have been disastrous. Heading the list of negative changes between then and now is the general practice of people not telling anyone the general area in which they are going. Instead, they seek anonymity, personal freedom, and concealed behaviors. While the democratic society does recognize and encourage individual privacy, there is nonetheless an intended destination or prospective location.

Because so many persons, especially youngsters, find this practice unacceptable, our sermon has been designed to address this need. The sermon is ungirded by the poetic statement "No man is an island unto himself." In this regard, the fact yet remains that people need people. The sermon will examine three aspects of the subject—knowing your whereabouts—namely: (1) to highlights this practice during colonial time, (2) to describe the changing pattern during contemporary times, and (3) to examine some biblical teachings about the value of knowing your whereabouts.

Since the first objective is historical in nature, the sermon format will exclude a section on history per se. instead, the emphasis will be placed on the first objective—knowing your whereabouts during colonial times and the accounts and sad the episodes of persons lost and/or killed during these times. With the wilderness, the wild beasts, the hostile Indians, and the times, the colonists, if they were to conquer the area, had to move; therefore, they followed the practice of telling someone where they were going and the anticipated time of their return. Many failed to return, but a search party was often able to locate them and even determine what had befallen them. Beloved, during those times, people were not so secretive about their actions; instead, they wanted to be found if lost. In general, their desires were realized because they had earlier informed someone regarding their whereabouts. Unfortunately, that pattern has undergone drastic changes nowadays.

This troubling fact leads to the second consideration—the secret involving one's whereabouts in modern society. It is troubling fact that our society has become so impersonal that next-door people do not know each other; husbands do not know the general location of their wives; wives have no general knowledge of their husband's whereabouts; and—sadness of all—too many parents have no earthly idea of where their children can be found.

In this child-oriented society of today, too many parents are timid, if not afraid, to ask their children where they can be found. Compounding the insecurity of parents is the fear to inquire as to what time their child will return home—the place where the parents pay the mortgage, the utilities, the phone bills, and the grocery. Friends, it doubtless sounds old fashioned to make an appeal for some meaningful communication between family member, yet this practice does have positive outcomes. In contrast, those persons who conceal their whereabouts often bring sadness to their family and even harm to themselves.

Lastly, let us now consider the final dimension of this subject—what does the Bible teach about knowing your whereabouts? There are many biblical references to the value of letting someone know your whereabouts. The Psalmist, recognizing the omnipresence or all-presence of God, wrote, "Whither shall I flee thy from presence If I take wings and fly to the air, Thou art there. Thou art there. Thou knoweth my down sitting and my uprising" (Ps. 139:7). Beloved, this scripture reminds us that although we may deceive our spouse or disrespect our parents, God had his eye on us, and Bible reminds us that we shall reap what we sow (Gal. 6:7).

The second Biblical reference on the value of someone knowing your whereabouts is found in the text of 1st Samuel 16:11. It is the account of the lad known as David. The Bible tells us that God instructed Samuel the prophet to go to Jesse's house and select one of his sons to become the next king of Israel. That was an honor for Jesse, so he immediately commenced to parade his sons before Samuel. Each one was rejected, but Samuel inquired, "Is this all of thy sons?" Jesse replied, "There remaineth the youngest one who is keeping the sheep." Samuel ordered them to go and bring David. Because David's father knew his whereabouts and David were in his place, his brothers could easily locate him; they brought him to Samuel who declared that this was the one whom the Lord would have him anoint as the next king of Israel. In closing, what a glorious honor befell David who became a great king, an illustrious poet, and whose lineage would include the ultimate birth of Christ.

Young people specifically and adults in general, let us adopt the practice of letting someone know our whereabouts. Remember, God already knows where we are, but we need someone to help pinpoint out earthly locations. Amen.

Chapter 16

The Young Dreamer

> And Joseph dreamed a dream, and he told it his brethren: And they hated him, and would not speak peaceably unto him.
>
> —Genesis 3:7–5

The normal human mind is a precious gift from God. It is the core of some of activities ranging from thought to action. Although it is part of the biological nature, the mind must be nurtured in its development after birth. It is, therefore, essential for parents and relatives to provide a structured set of ongoing stimulations to aid the child in its mental development. The sociologist refers to this process as socialization, but the lay person merely calls it good home training. In addition to the family, there are other sources of stimulation for mental development; some of these are relatives, playmates, schoolmates, and the church family. While all of those individuals help in the mental development of the young child, there is the basic God-given capacity that will determine the nature and scope of a person's mental activity. There is one aspect of the mind that manifests itself naturally or at least by divine energy, and it is the ability to dream or picture one's self in future situations. The reference herein is not to events that occur at night while asleep. Instead, it embraces divine insights, impressions, a vision of what one feels driven to seek.

Our sermon, in this connection, will be undergirded by that type of dream. Since these experiences often start early in life, the sermon has been entitled "The Young Dreamer." It will briefly examine three aspects of a young dreamer, namely: when to start dreaming, resentment toward the dreamer, and the positive outcomes of dreams. To enrich appreciation for the sermon, attention will be first focused on the textual anchor. It is found in Genesis 3:7 where the account is recorded of a youngster, Joseph the gifted dreamer. He was born when his father was well into age; therefore, he became the favorite son. His father gave him a coat of many colors; and this created hatred toward him from his brothers. The coat and his dreams became a problem for Joseph, but in due time, the dreams became realities.

Against this brief scriptural account, let us now turn attention to the earlier specified aspects of the sermon, the first of which is when to start dreaming. Friends, the tie to start dreaming is when one recognizes that ideas, pictures, and prospects start and continue to reappear in the mind. As a caution, however, the person must be sure that these stimulations come from within, and not from drugs! If these dreams continue to reappear, one can be sure that they are from above, and the master is trying to get the person's attention. Such was the experience of Joseph who, as a youngest had vivid reams about himself in relation to his family. Accordingly, he shared the dreams with his brothers, and of course, they rejected them.

This reaction of his brothers leads to the second aspect of our sermon; it is that resentment toward the dreamer. Young people specifically, and adults in general, let me remind you of a somber fact. People tend not to appreciate hearing of dreams, especially if they contain some negative information about them. In contrast, if they feel that your dream might help them to win in the lottery, they gladly welcome your information. In the textual account today, Joseph's brothers resented him because off his colorful coat, his father's affection for him, and his ability to have dreams. This was the situation when Joseph told his brothers about a dream in which his plants stood taller than theirs; the dislike was intensified when he further deepened their anger, and they made plans to rid themselves of the young dreamer. Eventually, the opportunity came, and the brothers took Joseph and placed him into a pit. They took his coat, soaked it in blood of a slain animal, carried it back to their father, and told him that Joseph was rescued and sold into slavery were Joseph continued to have dreams.

Later in Egypt, Joseph the dreamer was elevated to overseer, and a few years later his brothers came to Egypt in quest for grains. Friends, they knew it not but they were facing their brother Joseph—a divine fact that leads to the final concern of the sermon. It is the positive, often delayed, outcomes of having, believing, and following one's dream.

Young Joseph had told his brothers of his dream. He had told his father of his dream, and all of them thought that he was somewhat strange. Oh! He was shocked to be placed in a pit. He was disturbed by being sold into slavery. He was saddened by being falsely imprisoned in Egypt, but in due time he witnessed the reality of his dreams about his family. Joseph lived to see his brothers come to him in search of food, he lived to see his younger brother be brought to him, he lived to see his elderly father be brought to him, and he lived to face his brothers and tell them, "Come close. I am Joseph, your brother."

Friends, he wept as he told them, "You intended it for evil, but God intended it for good." So, in closing, beloved, never become too critical of dreams that young people have; instead, listen to them, see that dreams stem from above, and if so, help the child to nurture them. And remember, God is yet fillings our young children with dreams.

Chapter 17

The Haughty Son

> Children, obey your parents in the Lord: For this right.
>
> —Ephesians 6:1

The month of June contains two family-oriented Sundays, which are Youth Day and Father's Day. The former is observed on the second Sunday while the latter is noted on the third Sunday. In keeping with those calendar-specified days, the sermon topic today will focus on the youth. It has been entitled "The Haughty Child" and will explore three aspects of the subject, namely: the contemporary youth culture, biblical teachings on youth behavior, and some negative consequences of being haughty.

Prior to address these aspects of the subject, brief attention will be devoted to the scriptural anchors; they are two in number, one from the New Testament and the other from the Old Testament. The references are presented in the reverse order of their appearance in the Bible since the scriptural anchors come from the New Testament. Further, the negative outcomes of being haughty will be illustrated by an Old Testament personality.

With this synopsis of the scriptural anchors, attention will now be turned to the earlier specified objectives, the first one being the contemporary youth culture. Prior to the late 1960's, the youth culture was family oriented. Parents were decision makers, providers, disciplinarians, and objects of respect. Youth in the meantime were obedient, respectful, helpful, and functioned as team players. With the array of changes, laws, and new practices of the late '60's and becoming more prominent durn the '70's, there occurred a major change in the youth attitudes and practices with the family. They're occurred a near domino effect in the traditional youth perception of function with the family. Numerous were the changes, some of which were a rapid rise in individuality, the pursuit of instant gratification, a decline in respect for parents along with others in authority, earlier sexual experiences, and even a venture into vices of alcohol, drugs, and smoking. In addition to these new challenges to traditional family respect, there appeared two other potent forces, which were child abuse laws and the telecommunication revolution, the latter of which gave youth worldwide contacts. With the cell phone, youth have found a space outside of the home; it is called Myspace.

Beloved, this elaboration is a mere superficial presentation of how the youth culture is undermining traditional family values and, at the same time, contributing to a new lost generation, especially in minority families. At the same time, it is an incentive for children to be disobedient, disrespectful, and unfortunately a negative statistic in the job market but a great potential for the correctional system all because they are prone to be both disobedient and haughty.

This sad reality leads to the second aspect of the sermon, which is biblical teachings on the appropriate youth behavior. Starting with the Ten Commandments also known as the dialogues, there are many biblical teachings on youth behavior towards parents. In Exodus 19:12, it is recorded, "Honor thy father and thy mother, that thy days may be long upon the land which the Lord thy God giveth thee." In writing to the Corinthians, Paul stated, "When I was a child, I speak as a child, I understood as a child, I thought as a child, but when I became a man, I put away childless things" (1st Cor. 13:11). In a later letter to the Ephesians, Paul again wrote about childhood behavior as reflected in the words, "Children, obey your parents in the Lord, for this is right" (Ephesians 6:1).

Beloved, these three scriptural teachings, if followed, will enhance family life, promote ethical behavior, and be pleasing in the sight of God. Unfortunately, such actions are often not practices, and this neglect causes negative consequences that leads to the final aspects of the text—negative consequences for the disobedient youth who is often haughty as well. To be disobedient means to disregard orders, request, and suggestions from a person who is in authority. The word *haughty* carries a deeper meaning; it provides a hidden explanation for the neglect to be obedient, which is the person is blatantly and disdainfully proud. Unfortunately, such an individual is either unaware of or indifferent to the scriptural teaching "Pride goes before destruction and a haughty spirit before a fall" (Pr. 16:18).

Another scriptural citation that signals warning to disobedient youth is "be not deceived: God is not mocked: For whatsoever a man soweth, that shall he also reap" (Gal. 6:7). Using these scriptures along with the account of an Old Testament personality, Absalom, a brief narrative is herein presented to dramatize the negative outcome of being disobedient and haughty. It is embodied in the life of Absalom, the third child of David. He is described in the *Schofeld Study Bible* (529) as being "spoiled, impatient and overly ambitious." He was overzealous in his personal plot to have Amnon killed for having raped his siter, he was proud of his physical statue, and he was envious of his father's power. For a period, Absalom was feasting on the luster of apparent power; however, he would soon have to confront the negative consequence of being haughty and/or disobedient. The closing episode of Absalom's life is recorded in 2nd Samuel, chapter 18, verse 9. Therein are the following words recorded:" And Absalom rode upon a mule, and the mule went under the thick boughs of a great oak, and his head caught hold of the oak, and he was taken up between the heaven and the earth; and the mule that was under him went away." Hanging helpless, Absalom was killed by Joab. When his father, David heard of the death, he grieved and uttered, "O my son, Absalom, my son, my son, Absalom! Would God! I had died for thee, O Absalom my son, my son" (2nd Sam. 18:23).

In closing young people, never forget that someone was responsible for your coming int this world. Hopefully, those persons have jointly provided for you so don't become too arrogant, unappreciative, and indifferent to their teachings. Admittedly, this contemporary culture can so easily lure you away from the family, but you must never forget biblical teachings about your obligations as you move from being a child to becoming an adult. Lastly, do not let your self-image be like that of Absalom because you too can easily get caught under the oak tree of reality. Amen.

Chapter 18

The Children of Light

> For ye were sometimes darkness, but now are ye Light in the Lord: Walk as children of light.
>
> —Ephesians 5:8

The human life starts with a process called birth. At that time, the individual is known as a child. From birth to eighteen years of age, the individual goes through the stages of infancy, childhood, and adolescence. During that sojourn of eighteen years, the child has numerous experiences that will hold its basic personality structure. Among the crucial experiences are learning to walk, talk, read, and become goal conscious. While all of these experiences are essential for normal human existence, the ability to walk is of extreme importance for personal growth and development. The ability to walk can move an individual along on various pathways. Unfortunately, not all of the pathways are socially appropriate, for many leads to undesirable consequences.

The Bible, in this connection, has references to a two-pronged outcome of walking. One was spoken by Jesus who talked about walking on the broad way or the straight and narrow path (Matthew 7:14) and the other, our text today, was Paul's challenge to the Ephesians: he called on them to walk as children of light and not darkness (Ephesians 5:8). Since this Pauline contrast has implications both in worldly and spiritual affairs, our sermon was prepared to address this issue of walking from Paul's view. It was, therefore, entitled "Children of Light." The sermon will explore three dimensions of being children of light, namely: physical darkness versus light, spiritual darkness versus light, and expectations of those walking as children of light.

Prior to examining these aspects of being children of light, attention will be focused on the concepts of darkness and light. These words appear many times in the Bible, first in Genesis 1:3-5 where it is recorded that God divided the light from the darkness and, lastly, in Revelation 22:5 where it is noted that "there shall be no more night there…for the Lord God giveth them light."

The Bible also illustrates the value of slight for human welfare. During the Israelites journey from Egypt to the promised Land. God provided the pillar of fire to guide them during the night (Exodus 13:21). Years after the wilderness journey, David wrote about the value of light as noted in Psalm 119:105: "Thou word is a lamp unto my feet, and a light unto my path."

This symbolism of light continued into the New Testament, one example of which was the reference where Jesus referred to himself as the light of the world (John 8:12).

Friends, these few citations show the prevalence of darkness and the value of light for human welfare. The recognition of darkness and the need for light have been a constant experience throughout human history. This fact leads to the first consideration of the text, which is physical darkness versus light. Starting with god's division of time into night and day, human activity has been impaired by the absence of light. Admittedly, night or darkness is intended as a time for relaxation, rest and rejuvenation. Humankind has nonetheless craved light for movement both outside and within the dwelling place. Accordingly, people have devised methods many different means to produce light. These efforts have included the open fire, candles, fireplace, oil lamps, flashlights, electric lights, and laser beams since those early efforts, humanity has devised methods to almost transform night into day. While the lighting of night is a spectacular accomplishment, the fact remains that light is indispensable for growth and development of both plant and animal life. Hence, there is an ongoing need of light for the continuance of civilization. The challenge, in this connection, is for us to maximize the use of night or darkness for study, rest, and sleep to be prepared for meeting the demands contained in the day of light.

This truism leads to the second facet of our sermon; it is that of spiritual darkness versus spiritual light. The Bible used darkness as a symbol of total depravity during Old Testament history. Within that state of existence, humankind was alienated from God. That theme of darkness continued into the New Testament but with a slightly different meaning; it was that of deliberate sinful life rather than submitting to the forgiveness of transgressions made possible by the atoning blood of Jesus. The account of Bartimaeus—the person born blind—is a lucid example of darkness versus light. Upon receiving his sight, Bartimaeus later said, "Whereas I was blind, I now see." Friends, until a person acknowledges his sinfulness and seeks forgiveness from Jesus as Lord and Savior, that individual is living in spiritually darkness. In contrast, a person has merely to "confess with thy mouth the Lord Jesus, and shalt believe in thine heart that God hath raised him from the dead, thou shalt be saved" (Romans 10:9), a process that transforms one from spiritual darkness to spiritual light. Beloved, this conversion experience is the mere beginning of living the new life, for the bible tells us that "if any man be in Christ Jesus, he is anew creature: old things are passed away, behold, all things are become new" (2nd Corinthians 5:17).

This biblical affirmation leads to the final consideration of the sermon, which is expectations of those who are walking as children of light. It has a twofold level of application, one for the daily obligations of children and the other for adult Christians. Let us consider the young people first. To be viewed as children of light requires you to be obedient to those in authority, respectful of parents, adults, and the elderly, be diligent in fulfilling your schoolwork obligations, perform household duties as assigned, avoid delinquent behavior, be honest, dream of and work toward becoming successful persons, develop the habit of praying, be a participant in church activities, and be kind toward one another. Remember, Jesus placed great emphasis on children. On one occasion, Jesus said, "Except you be converted, and become as little children, ye shall not enter into the kingdom of heaven (Matthew 18:3). The soul-searching question facing you, our young people today is. Could Jesus have used you in his child-text sermon?

Lastly, let us look at Paul's description of adults who were walking in the darkness rather than as children of light. Kindly refer to chapter 5 of Ephesians verse 1-8 and let us examine the wide range of behaviors involving those adults who are children of darkness. Oh, beloved, persons guilty of any of these transgressions need not be permanently lost because there is yet the transforming power in the redemptive blood of Christ. In this regard, John 3:16 echoes a beam of hope; it states that "God so loved the world that he gave his only begotten Son that whosoever believes in him should not perish, but have everlasting life."

In closing, the common question facing all of us is What will be the theme of our life when we walk the last mile of the way? Will it be one of darkness or one of light? My humble prayer is that we shall all be labeled as children of light. Amen.

Chapter 19

The Toils and Rewards of Study

—2nd Tim.2:15

The philosopher John Locke asserted that at birth, the human mind is like a clean chalkboard. The babe is therefore devoid of all knowledge. Soon after birth, however, an extensive nurturing process commences; it includes food, clothing, personal care, and communication to the infant. From that initial process onward, the child will undergo a series of stimuli known as socialization. That process is designed to transform the little biological being into a socialized person. Initially, that training process occurs in the family, but in the process of time, it extends beyond that unit into a more formalized setting known as formal education. Whereas the family is informal and much of the training is either by word of mouth or imitation of the parents, the school system, being formal, has a more rigorous procedure for imparting knowledge. It is one that requires study to hear, understand, participate in discussions, and to pass the required courses. Accordingly, the central concept in education is that od study. The call for study extends beyond the school system as noted in the scripture earlier read. Therein, an admonition is given to study for both knowledge and proficiency in utilizing and dispensing of information. That scripture, 2nd Timothy 2:15, will be used to undergird the sermon entitled "The Toils and rewards of Study."

This subject is deemed appropriate and timely since today is our Annual Awards and Recognition Worship here at Institutional First Baptist Church. The sermon will address the following dimensions of the subject, namely: the need for study, some challenges in study, prerequisites for study, and rewards from study. Prior to examining the four concerns, brief attention will be given to the textual anchor of the sermon. It was written by Paul to his son in the ministry, Timothy. In terms of hermeneutics, the word *study* as used herein does not refer to the traditional classroom study. As noted in the *King James Bible Commentary*, study is not the normal word you think of as student but a word used of a workman meaning 'give diligence,' 'endeavor,' or 'exerts oneself' (to show approved unto God).

Study, as used in the sermon today, will be a slight variance from the theological stance and, thereby, assume as academic focus with the emphasis being placed on diligence in pursuing formal education. With this operational definition of *study* attention will now be directed to the first division of the sermon, which is the need for study. It is through study that the biological being is transformed into a socialized individual. Through this lengthy process, the individual learns essential parts of its culture; it acquires specialized knowledge in some areas of life and, therefore, becomes recognized as an intelligent being. Through study, a person can attain personal, mental, social, and spiritual development. Paul, in his message to the Thessalonians, seems to have placed emphasis on study for personal development and work as reflected in the words, "And that you study to be quiet, and to do your own business, and to work with your own hands, as we have commanded you" (1st Thess. 4:11).

This Pauline teaching leads to the second component of the sermon, which is the challenge of study. Beloved, it is an unfortunate fact that the vastness of publications now poses a selection problem for many people, especially the young readers.

The pulp entertainment, juvenile, and self-enhancement publications all draw wider readership than academic, literary, geographical, and religious sources. While reading is a personal matter, it must be recognized, however, that the ultimate test will come when each individual is assessed by academic and/or employment measurements. At that time, there is often a high attrition or fallout. The Bible, in an Old Testament warning, describes such a reality in the words, "My people are destroyed for a from a lack of knowledge" (Hosea 4:6). Young people and all others here assembled, let us survive to avoid Hosea's indictment from becoming our epithet.

This somber assessment leads to the third division of the sermon; it is prerequisites for study. Beloved, this word—*prerequisites*—is just a big word used instead of *requirements*. However, the concerns remain the same irrespective of which word used. Instead of drawing from psychology and human development to gleam insights, the study will be restricted to one role model. It is found in the Bible where a description of Jesus was recorded in Luke 2:40. Therein it is noted, "And the child grew, and waxed strong in spirit, filled with wisdom: and the grace of God was upon him." Beloved, within that one verse is a cogent description of the requirements for effective study. They are all embodied in the growth of Jesus who is herein presented as the role model for study preparation. Within that verse is found a trilogy of requirements; they are physical growth, mental growth, and spiritual growth. These three areas signify the need for bodily growth, intellectual expansion, and spiritual development. Collectively, they are influenced by lifestyle, reading along with educational exposure, and spiritual experiences engendered by prayer and cooperative worship.

Having identified the desirable role model for study, the final concern becomes that of rewards for study. Since rewards tend to be viewed as by-product for earlier endeavors, it can be concluded that effective stud engenders rewards for the dedicated and successful individuals. While the rewards are numerous, the sermon will be confined to only four types. Since the human mind is the locus for thinking, comprehending, storing, recalling, and coordinating movement, the growth in intellectual capacity is without doubt a cherished reward from study.

Chapter 20

Obedience: Its Obligations and Rewards

> Children obey your parents in the Lord: for this is right.
>
> —Eph. 6:1

The family is one of the basic units of society. It consists of at least two generations, parents, and at least one child. It is responsible for reproduction and rearing of children. Historically, the family was diligent, positive and compassionate in the childrearing process. Similarly, the children were respectful, helpful and obedient. This family style was the theme of several television programs during the last quarter of the twentieth century. Unfortunately, that compassionate family style has been uprooted by the World Wide Web, cell phones, the iPad and an array of social network sites. Some of the negative outcomes engendered by this twenty-first-century lifestyle are self-interest, disregard for others, and disobedience. It is the latter reality that will be the focus of today's sermon, especially for the Scouts but all others who are here gathered. The sermon has been entitled, "Obedience, Obligations and Rewards". It will include three considerations, namely: (a) the obligations of children, (b) the obligations of adults, and (c) obligations of everybody.

As a background for the analysis, attention will be focused on two words that undergird the subject; they are *obedience* and *rewards*. The word *obedience* denotes the willingness to listen, obey, comply with, and diligently follow instructions given by one who is in charge. It is a significant part of the growing-up process and will become increasingly important following the childhood stage. The Bible depicts Jesus as being obedient both as a child and later as an adult. It shows Jesus as a child going with his foster father, Joseph, and mother going to the temple. (Lk. 2:21-24), and later working as a carpenter in Joseph shop (Mk.6:3).

The next background word is *reward*. As defined by *Webster*, it denotes something that is given in return for an action committed. A reward can be given for a positive action, but it can also be issued for a negative or bad action. The Bible has numerous teachings about both types of rewards. Against this background on the word *obedience* and *reward,* attention will now be directed to the earlier is specified three components of the subject, the first of which is the obligations of children.

As noted in the text, Paul called upon children to obey their parents in the Lord, for this is right. This obligation will diligently fulfill for many years; however, it seems to becoming something of the past. Sadly, this deviation is more prevalent in minority that in the majority families. It is herein submitted that too many parents are placing little, if any, pressure on children to be obedient. The unfortunate fact is that they both will receive negative experiences; first the parents and later the children. The over permissive parents are merely promoting disrespect and even contempt from their children. The Bible in this regard, warns such children that they shall reap what they sow. In contrast, the families in which the children are obedient, respectful and cordial are promised a positive reward. In support of this assertion, reference is called to the Bible in which it is taught. "Honor thy father and thy mother in order that thy days will be longer upon the land that the Lord giveth thee."

This fact leads to the second dimension of this sermon—the obligations of parents and the resulting rewards. In keeping this biblical tradition, the father is called upon "to provoke not your children to wrath: Bring the up in the nurtured and admonition of the Lord" (Ep.6:4). In another biblical reference, the father is called upon to provide food, not a stone but bread for these children, and in so doing, he will be emulating the Heavenly Father who gives good gifts. In an Old Testament account, a mother is described as taking care of the household and being concerned about her children. In the end, according to the Bible, she will receive a positive reward as recorded in Pr. 32:28. "Her children arise up, and call her blessed; her husband also and he praiseth her."

This biblical assertion leads to the final consideration of this sermon; it is obligations of everybody. While there are numerous obligations from which one be excluded because of age, health, economic status, there does remain one that applies to the whole of humanity with the Christian community. It is that of believing in the Bible as a recorded word of God written by "holy men of God speak as they were moved by the Holy Ghost" (2nd Peter 1: 21). Within that sacred script are found in array of teachings that we should embrace and obey. Just a few of them will be enumerated. God is Eternal Absolute; it is impossible to escape from the presence of God; God sent his only begotten Son, in order that believing humankind can receive reward of salvation; Jesus died on Calvary to pay the sin price for salvation; humankind is a sinner by nature but can achieve forgiveness in recorded in Romans 10:9; life is a transitory journey; the ultimate judgment will come. These biblical certainties leave us with the question as the Philippian jailer, "What must I so to be saved? It is herein submitted that four obligations are essential: believe in the Bible, hide its word into your heart, be converted and be faithful unto death.

Finally, being obedient to these biblical teachings will lead to the reward of eternal as promised by Jesus: "Be thou faithful unto death and I will give thee a crown of life" (Rev.2:10).

Amen.

Chapter 21

Benefits of Obedient Children

> Children, obey your parents in the Lord, for this is the right. Honor thy father, and mother; which is the first commandment with promise: that it may be well with thee, and thou mayest live long on the earth.
>
> —Ephesians 6:1–3

Physicians, biologist, and even laymen agree that the human birth process yields a little animal. Without an extensive nurturing period, the little animal would never become a socialized person. Much has been written about the need for and value of training in the development of a normal personality. Freud, four examples, suggests that the human psyche moves through three stages, the latter being known as the superego. He described that final stage as one in which the individual has attained an awareness of right and wrong and recognizes the existence of rules and regulations. It is also the stage in which the person respects those in authority and freely abides by existing regulations. Such an individual is referred to as being properly socialized or as having good home training. Undergirding the nature of home training is the child's willingness to be obedient.

This emphasis on obedience is a theme in both the Old and New Testament; however, it is often neglected in present day society. Unfortunately, this neglect starts in the home, or should I say house. It erodes into the school system, it invades the workforce, and it disregards religious teachings.

Admittedly, Western society places much emphasis on freedom of expression and individual choices, but it fails to properly warn of the downside of disobedience. Our sermon, in this connection, has been planned to address the topic of obedience. The undergirding objective is to alert our young people, specifically of the critical need to be obedient, and warn them of impending dangers in being disobedient. The sermon will explore the following dimensions of obedience.

> the current state of affairs ass result of disobedience
> critical areas in which obedience is needed
> some negative outcomes of this obedience

As background for the analysis, attention will be focused on the concept of obedience. This word can be defined as an act or instance of obeying; it also means observing and complying with rules and regulations. Obedience is a core expectation in the childrearing process, and it has a way of being recognized positively or negatively in human action.

Against this background on obedience, let us now focus on the first consideration, which is the current state of affairs involving human activities. Even a casual glance of daily affairs discloses action of disobedient individuals. Nowadays, children are controlling, if not reshaping, their parents. They are disobedient, selfish, hostile, and indifferent to good manners. Numerous are the children who run the family and even try to exercise the same authority outside the home. Sadly, the more disobedient is a child, the greater is the probably of delinquent behavior. Remember, the Bible teaches that charity begins at home and spreads abroad; In a similar manner, disobedience begins at home as spread abroad.

Beloved, the over permissiveness of our parents is having a negative effect on the welfare of our children. Statistics of alternative school enrollment, YDC confinement, juvenile detention, drug involvement, early sexuality, and even homicidal activities all point back to laxity in the home with respect to obedience. Without attempting to submit programs to change this problem of disobedience in the home, suffice it to indicate that the first effort must be made in the home. The second consideration of obedience is the question of what areas should it be practiced. It is herein suggested that there are three areas the first of which is the family. This area was highlighted in the earlier description of disobedience. However, it can be added that obedience in the family leads to respect, mutual aid, family concerns, and goodwill. Additionally, obedience helps to make a house become at home. To assure the presence of obedience in the family, the parent or parents must commence the training process at an early age. Further, they must be consistently positive in demanding obedience from the children. The call is not for corporal punishment; instead, it is a plea for alternative methods such as home confinement, budgetary restraints, and legal removal of the disobedient child from the home.

The next need area for obedience is the school system. Beloved, our school are becoming jungles perpetuated largely by our children of color. The kids are loud, disrespectful, skilled in profanity and nearly ignorant in English, belligerent in the hall, disrespectful of the teachers, and quick to start a fight. While all these problems are mounting, the decision makers—largely white—are allowing the computerized record to keep a trail of the troublemaker who soon will be removed from the system. Friends, it is such an irony to find parents who want to whip the teacher for confronting the disobedient child. It is a shame that the parent cannot be whipped for early, neglecting the demand obedience from the child.

The third area in which obedience is expected is that of Christianity. The Holy Bible calls upon all people to be obedient to its teaching. Of particular concern today is the call to children. Our text, for example, instructs children; it states "Children, obey your parents in the Lord: for this is right" (Eph.6:1). Included in the Ten Commandments is the instruction to obey parents. The statement is "Honor thy father and thy mother" (Exodus 20:12). This emphasis on honoring parents was both practice and taught by Jesus. On one occasion, he said that whosoever doeth the will of his Father who is in heaven is his brother and his sister.

As we come to the end of our sermon, the final consideration is twofold. First is the question of what are some positive outcomes from being obedient to our parents. Let us hear the Bible speak on this question. In the Old Testament, we are told that our days will be long upon the land that the Lord giveth us. A similar promise in echoed in the text, '" Children, obey your parents in the Lord: for this is right." Paul also stated that things will go well with us, and we will experience long life. In addition to these divine promises, I add a social consequence from being obedient to our parents—we will merit their good wishes, symbolize their desires for us, and be the answers to their prayers for our welfare.

The second aspect of this last consideration is that of negative outcome from being disobedient. It can range from being disinherited by the family, expelled from school, imprisoned, to divinely punished by God. Beloved, the last one—divine punishment—is the most severe.

The life of Absalom is a lucid example of discord in the family. Absalom was a charming and handsome person from the sole of his foot to the crown over his head. Sadly, he became overly ambitious even to the point of challenging the authority of his father. The episode of Absalom's cunningness ended with his hair being caught on a tree limb and left hanging as the horse did not stop. His father's grief was expressed in the words, "O my son, Absalom, my son, my son Absalom! Would God I had died for thee, O, Absalom, my son, my son" (II Samuel19:33).

In closing, young people, the Bible is yet true—honor thy father and mother. Children will be your parents, and you will be blessed in so complying with parental instruction, honored in your community, and disciplined for the journey of life. Amen.

Chapter 22

The Frazzled Sister

> Marta, Martha, you are worried and trouble about many things, but one thing is needed, and Mary has chosen that good part which will not be taken away from her.
>
> —Luke 10: 41–42

The daily toils of life place heavy demands on the human body; these demands cause physical fatigue, mental stress, psychological abnormalities, sleep disorders, and temperamental extremities. Although these daily toilets exist throughout the year, they are more prevalent at times that include Christmas shopping, holiday weekends, preparation for a wedding, and school-related activities. Probably the most pervasive time is the beginning of the new school year. As is well-known by both parents and children. The chores of preparing for school are varied, expensive, and energy draining. School supplies, school uniforms, appropriate documents, bus route, after-school care all can so easily cause parents and students to become frazzled.

Our sermon, in this connection, has been planned to address this problem; it has been entitled "The Frazzled Sister." The sermon is anchored by three objectives, namely:

1. to highlight fatigue as a consequence of being frazzled

2. to specify some marks of being frazzled
3. to present the biblical method to offset the problem of becoming frazzled.

Where us our traditional sermon format includes background highlights, the presentation today will bypass that emphasis and move to the first objective that includes historical dimensions; that objective is to highlight fatigue as a consequence of being frazzled. Prior to exploring aspects of this objective, attention will be placed on the keyword of the sermon; it is that of *frazzled*. This word denotes the setting in which one is in a state of extreme nervous fatigue; it can also be viewed as constant bewilderment; further, frazzled denotes indecisiveness, a general tendency to overreact, constant worry about self in relation to others, and a recurring period of self-pity. In sum, to be frazzled means that such an individual feels helmed in, unsure about decisions, and nearly ready to symbolically throw in the towel. Such a situation invariably causes a feeling of fatigue.

In this connection, let us now turn to the problem of fatigue. It is generally known that fatigue is one of our most common complaints. Too many people are juggling multiple responsibilities while getting too little sleep and not enough exercise. It is generally known that the operator fatigue is the main cause of most accidents whether land, sea or air. Although strict laws are being coded to protect the American public from traveling hazards associated with fatigue, there is a more cogent type of fatigue that laws cannot correct. That type of fatigue, also known as being frazzled, is personal; it's like the proverbial shadow; it goes in and out with each person, and it can quickly ebb away self-confidence. Unfortunately, many frazzled persons are so victimized by their personal mind-set rather than actions of others or restrictions by society. A lucid biblical case to support this assertion is found in our text today. Therein Jesus met a frazzled woman and talked to her about her condition. Her name was Martha; she had a sister named Mary whose perception on life was just the opposite of hers; the sisters lived in a town of Bethany, just outside Jerusalem. Martha was hard-working and caring in her daily pursuits, but she was frazzled; she had not one but five overlapping problems.

Let us see what the Bible tells us about Martha's problems. First, she was distracted. Versus 39-40 say "But Martha was distracted with much serving. These verses merely mean that Martha was pulled in every direction. Can any of us identify with Martha? Do we allow ourselves to become too busy, busier than God intends, busier than necessary, busier than wise? If so, that is why we are so often tired or fatigue. Martha was, secondly, plagued by the problem of doubting. Verse 40 tells us that she inquired, "Lord do you not care?" How often, while being pulled in all direction, do we momentarily doubt God's caring and concern? Martha's concern was an echo of David, who wrote, "No one cares for my soul" (Ps 142:4). But they were both in error because Jesus does care! When one begins to feel that the Lord does not care, that person is experiencing the third problem of Martha; it is a feeling of self-pity.

Let us listen in on Martha's complaint to the Lord. She said, "Lord, do you not care that my sister has left me the serve alone?" Of course, Martha did need help. No one denies that. Many hands make light work. The running of a household and the entertaining of guest require that every member of the family does her/his part. But Martha's agenda did not line up with the agenda of the Master. He wanted Martha to first praise him and then pursue her goals. That she did not do; therefore, Martha had a fourth problem. It was that of worrying. The Lord was aware of her worry, and He said onto her "Martha, Martha, you are worried."

Friends, she was worried, but Martha had brought it on herself. She was busybody. She wanted to do everything. She wanted to hear everything, and eventually, her energy was depleted.

Lastly, Martha was troubled because she had become exhausted while her sister, Mary, was composed and listening to the teachings of Jesus. Remember, she too has been in the company of the Master, but Martha chose to be the industrious person as if to impress Jesus. Beloved, let us remember to avoid that stance of Martha, and choose, rather, to be like her sister Mary presented in the Bible as placing Christ first in her life. She was not frazzled as was her sister, Martha; instead, she was composed.

In closing our sermon, a few words will now be addressed to our schoolchildren. Young people I call upon you to avoid becoming frazzled in the school situation. Recognize that you may perform better in some subjects and extracurricular activities than others. Devote a little more time to the problem situations while continuing to excel in the areas of your competency. Lastly, make a commitment to remain in school, and in so doing you will be like Mary who sat at the feet of Jesus. So, as said Jesus to Martha—to paraphrase—"Martha, you are worrying about the wrong things while Mary, your sister, has chosen that good part, which cannot be taken away from her." Young people, complete your education because it, like Mary's experience, cannot be taken away from you. Amen.

Chapter 23

The spiritual values of grandparents

> When I call the remembrance of unfeigned faith that is in thee which dwelt first in thy grandmother Lois, and thy mother Eunice; and I am persuaded that in thee also
>
> —2nd Timothy 1:5

Most societies consist of five distinct set of values, actions, and rules. Collectively, these values, actions and rules are known as institutions. The social scientist has classified the institutions into five types which are religion, family, education, government, and economic. Religion is viewed as the oldest since it embodies knowledge about God and creation. The family is next because it was a divine creation as recorded in Genesis (1: 26-27).

That first family consisted of Adam, Eve, Cain, Abel and later Seth. Theologically, Adam became the federal head of the human race, and it, irrespective of differences in statue, color, language and location embodies the line age of Adam. From the time of Adam and Eve to this day and age, the human group has reproduced offspring. This reproduction process can be viewed across generational lines; hence, there are children, parents, grandparents, and in contemporary times, great-grandparents.

The Bible contains example of grandparents, both males and females. Our sermon today, in observation of National Grandparents' Day, has been entitled "The Spiritual Value of Grandparents." While acknowledging that there are biblical accounts of the grandfather, the emphasis in this sermon will be placed on the grandmother. It will explore three roles or activities of the grandmother, namely: essential functions of the grandmother, challenges that confront the grandmother, and the downside of being a grandmother.

Prior to addressing these three aspects the grandmother experiences, attention will be focused on the word *grandmother*. It refers to a female of the third generation: first there is the child, secondly, there is the mother, and thirdly there is the mother of either the child's mother or father. Whenever the three generations share the same house, the unit is called an extended family. Although there were many examples of grandmothers in biblical history, the word *grandmother*, according to *Strong's Concordance* occurs only once in the Bible (see Strong's definition number 3125). As noted in the text, the word *grandmother* was used in Paul's message to Timothy (2nd Timothy 1:5). This single reference should not be taken to mean that grandmothers were non-existent or even unimportant. Instead, the exclusion was representative of the male-dominated culture during biblical history.

A permanent example of grandmother's presence is the family of Abraham; it consisted of Sarah—his wife, Ishmael, and Isaac, his son; and Isaac married Rebekah and they became parents of Esau and Jacob. Within these three generations was Rebekah the mother of Esau and Jacob, and there was Sarah the grandmother of those two boys. Yet, there are no references to Sarah as grandmother, but numerous are the references to the grandfather configuration, the most frequent one being "the God of Abraham, Isaac, and Jacob." So, while the women give birth to the children, they were never highlighted in an intergeneration setting as a grandmother.

Against this synopsis of the word *grandmother*, let us now turn attention to the earlier-specified considerations on the grand-mother—the first one being essential functions of the grandmother. While the Bible is largely silent on the significance of grandmothers, family sociologist has written extensively on the roles of grandmothers. One in particular is Robert Ashley who in his book *An Introduction to Social Gerontology* identified several roles that grandparents can play with the family; he listed "just being their…family historians…crisis managers…arbitrators…role model…surrogate parents…and financial support." In addition to these functions, the research shows that grandparents can impart values to the grandchildren. Among the values are ethics, morality, and biblical teachings. While all of functions are important, our sermon will place major emphasis on the ethical, moral, and biblical teachings of grandmothers. These three areas are the foundation of character and the pathway to salvation by accepting Jesus as Lord and Savior.

It was within this last area, biblical teachings that Paul referenced in his message to Timothy. Remember that textual anchor in which Paul talked about the unfeigned faith of Timothy's grandmother and his mother. Within that verse is found Paul's sincere expectation of Timothy to demonstrate Christian values because of the household in which he was reared. Beloved, what an expectation! Leaping across the annual of time, what would be the assessment if it were possible for Paul to visit our grandmothers today? Would he find a similar commitment, or would he be in a stage of shock to find grandmothers cloaking for their granddaughters, using illicit drugs in the presence of the grandchildren, and being over permissive toward their grandchildren? Hopefully, he would find the compassionate-yet- stern grandmother whose unfeigned faith would be like that of the bewildered mother in *Raisin in the Sun*. Within that production was a young overzealous female who makes a derogatory statement about God. That elderly woman was distraught; she slapped the girl and then said, "Repeat after me. In my mother's house there is a God." Reluctantly, the young female said, "In my mother's house there is a God."

Friends this sermon is no advocacy to slap religious values into the head of youngsters. Now that is child abuse, it is instead a wakeup call for adults to start religious training at an early age, to live a Christian life before the children, and to regularly check on the religious activities of the children.

While grandparents can be a vital resource in the overall functioning of a family, there are some challenges that so often they must face. This fact leads to our second aspect of the sermon; it is that of challenges in being grandparents. Within a large segment of the underprivileged population, this problem is a special challenge for many African-American grandparents. Robert Staples in his book *The Black Family* identified two major problems those grandparents. One is the result of what he called the death of black motherhood. It comes from mothers in prostitution, drugs, and the delinquent subculture. They have babies and nearly abandon them. In the meantime, the grandmother must come to the rescue. The other problem stems from the adolescent girl becoming pregnant and her parents put her out of the house. Beloved, these two problems stem from low moral, ethical, and religious values. But thanks be to God, there is often the caring grandmother.

And now back to the posted sermon. While there are numerous challenges facing the grandparent, attention will be restricted to two of them. The first is that of how to balance personal concern with being supportive but not a replacement for the nonproductive parent. This problem is intensified by the fact that the grandparent's financial resources are restricted to Social Security and other governmental-entitlement sources. The second challenge is in the area of authority. Parents often find themselves being reported to the grandparents, especially when their children are unhappy with them. Within the situation, the grandparent has to walk a delicate line between her child and her grandchild. This tensed situation leads to the final consideration of the sermon; it is the downside of grandparenting.

Owing to the increasing life spans, it is possible for some grandparents to become great-grandparents. Ironically, many great grandparents are now responsible for another generation of children. In the meantime, they are facing three inescapable realities; the increasing disabilities caused by advancing age, the need to consider and make final plans for their end of life and above all to cling to the secured hand of the Lord and Savior Jesus Christ. Such elderly persons should echo the words. "O when I come to the end of life's journey. Weary of life, and the battle is won; caring the staff and the cross of redemption, He'll understand, and say "Well done."

Chapter 24

Facing Life

Remember now thy Creator.

—Ecclesiastes 12:1

Life is a short journey between birth and death. It starts with a struggle to activate the breezing process and ends when this activity that no longer be sustained. Life varies in length within the human group. Some individuals are blessed with longevity into the eighties; many pass the biblically defined seventy; and several expires in the sixties. At the other end, some individuals die during early childhood, some during the adolescent period, others in young adulthood. Irrespective of the age, when it happens, the Bible tells us, "It is appointed unto men once to die" (Hebrews 9: 27).

While great emphasis is placed on long life, it must be noted that the ultimate value of a life is viewed in terms of how it was used for self and others rather than the number of years a person lived. The challenge, in this connection, is that of structuring one's outlook on life at an early age. This is the message in our text today that is lifted from the twelfth chapter of Ecclesiastes. The first verse of that chapter will be used for our subject, facing life. The sermon is planned to encourage young people to begin thinking about the future role in life, and at the same time, to include an identification with the Creator. In keeping with the theme of Ecclesiastes, the sermon will draw three objectives from that writing, namely: the youth envisioning their future; the adults pursuing life goals, and the elderly coping with life.

As a brief scriptural highlights, Ecclesiastes is one of the five poetic books of the Bible; the other four are Job, Psalms, Proverbs, and the Songs of Solomon. These books are so designated because at times, they read like poetry, they form lyrics for songs, they reflect a literary style, and they focus on numerous dimensions of life. Ecclesiastes and the Songs of Solomon were written by King Solomon, a son of David and the third king of the United Kingdom of Israel. Solomon is described as the wisest man ever to live except Jesus Christ. In addition to his literary talent, King Solomon was a diplomat and a builder. It was under his leadership that the First Temple was built in Jerusalem. In the book of Ecclesiastes is found his reflection on youth while ebbing into old age; he, therefore, penned words of wisdom to the youth for guidance in their focusing on life.

Against this brief sketch on the textual writer, attention will now be turned to the earlier specified points of consideration, the first of which is youth envisioning their future. Life, for many young people, is like a crossword puzzle in which they are searching for meaningful words from amidst a collection of letters. It is a further, a time of experimental job seeking with confidence that their parents are available to sustain them. Additionally, young people are quick to feel that they are being overly supervised by their parents until trouble occurs. On the regrettable side, it is a fact that many young people are disrespectful of the parents and all other adults; they defiant, daring, and ultra-self-centered. As would be expected, such young people have little, if any, interest in religious matters. They completely neglect the textual call to "Remember now thy Creator, in the days of thy youth." So, instead of facing life, such young people are being driven by worldly vanity, peer pressure, and various delinquent groups. While this lifestyle may seem to offer inner satisfaction, my friends, it is bound to end in frustration. Such a disaster can be avoided by merely including self-respect, parental honor, and learning to be prayerful.

The text moves from the youth, secondly to the young adults without direct references to them as a category. It implies that they are busy, whether single or married, with responsibilities that include working, nurturing, protecting and trying to survive in an exploitative society. They struggle with mortgages, installments, household expenses, allowances for children, and concerns about retirement. With these wide ranges of concerns and responsibilities, it follows that young adults should heed the biblical admonition to the youth and, therefore, remember their Creator. This type of religious conviction will preclude using Sunday as a day for yard work, to relax, or to wash the family vehicle.

Solomon in Ecclesiastes, does allude to the elderly population. As noted, his description, the third period in life is that of coping with its increasing disabilities. He provides an extensive list of the decrements or health-related problems in the closing phase of life. In a symbolic way, Solomon identified age-related problems: (1) trembling limbs, hands, and fingers; (2) loss of accurate vision; (3) loss of teeth; (4) hearing loss; (5) prone to fall; and (6) impending death.

Admittedly, the middle age and we, elderly persons, have multiple age-related problems, but the glorious fact is that we can endure the toils and bear the pain supported by our faith in God whom we have remembered since our youth. We know and trust him, especially where he said, "I will never leave you, nor forsake you" (Josh. 1:5).

In closing, let all of us take a few moments to reflect on our relationship to the Almighty God. If any of you have not embraced this spiritual source, my prayer is for your mind to be changed. For those who remember the Creator, I commend you and pray for your commitment to remain and intensify. Lastly, I highly recommend that each of you will find time to read Ecclesiastes 12. May God bless and keep you.

Epilogue

The human family has undergone periods of stress and strain during various historical periods. It's form and function have and continue to be interrelated with factors that include religion, geographical location, political philosophy, and tolerance of the people. Accordingly, it is possible to identify four historical periods in which specific family types prevailed. The first historical period, using the Bible for documentation, is Creation. In terms of family life, Creation included a monogamous family structure; it consisted of one husband, Adam, and one white Eve, and their children Cain, Abel, and later Seth. That first family is the undergirding theme of this book on the Christian family.

Slavery in America was the second for studying family structure; its duration was from 1619 to 1865. In the initial phase of that system, rigorous codes and prohibitions were used to create a docile slave. The regulations include discontinuation of using the native language, no formal religious worships, and no recognition of earlier marriages in the native land. In the process of time, there did emerge a quasi-marriage of slaves; it consisted of jumping over the broomstick administered by the plantation owner or his appointee. This type of union was fragile in that the owner could separate any member of the unit at will for financial gains.

Thirdly, if the Russian experiment with elimination of the family structure within that country. According to historical accounts, the endeavor was a failure as was demonstrated when it was replaced during the Bolshevik Revolution.

Fourthly, and finally, the family structure in China, which for a number of years has been subjected to a single-child union. Obviously, this mandate is stressful for the couple who desires more than one child or has a preference for a male instead of a female child.

When consideration is given to these four historic types of family structures, it can be concluded that the Christian family is more congruent with the family type during Creation. Since that description is recorded in the Bible, and that book contains the origin, spread, doctrines, and foundations of Christianity, it is herein concluded that this study of the Christian family is anchored on sound theological teachings. It is the thesis of this book that the Christian family is a microcosm of the one established during Creation. In terms of structure, this family is monogamous as were Adam and Eve; it has children as did Adam and Eve, and it has specific gender roles as did Adam and eve. Whereas the union of Adam and Eve had divine sanction per se, the Christian family has multiple sanctions such as the legal one—a marriage license is required before the ceremony can be performed, usually in ecclesiastical official usually officiate at the wedding, and prayers are uttered at the marriage ceremony.

The Christian family herein encompasses a call for dedication of the husband/father, wife/mother, child/children, and grandparents. The family roles, in this regard, place responsibilities on each individual. The father is expected to be a good father and a righteous father; the mother must be a praying woman and one who prevails amidst trials and tribulations; the child/children should honor their parents, be obedient, and keep their parents informed about their whereabouts. Lastly, the family with grandparent(s) sharing the residence should utilize the spiritual values of those person(s) in the socialization and monitoring the grandchildren. Finally, the extent to which a family knows, believes, and actualized the teachings embodied in this book will determine—to a large extent—the level of love, confidence, and happiness that will prevail in the Christian family.

Sources

The Bible (KJV)
Dr. Sherman's Libraries

About The Author

Eugene G. Sherman, Jr., Ph.D., is a Purdue trained sociologist where he majored in sociology and minored in history. He is a professor emeritus of sociology from Albany State University in Albany, Georgia. He, also, holds two earned doctorate degrees (in Scared Theology and the other in Religious Studies)/ dr. Sherman's religious experiences include: Organizing Institutional First Baptist Church of Albany, Georgia in 1971; Executive Dean of the Albany Center of Bethany Divinity College and Seminary; Dothan, Alabama (1988-2011) and Adjunct Professor of Religious History at Beulah Heights University; Atlanta, Georgia (2009- 2011). Since June of 2007, he has posted his weekly sermon on www.biblicalechoes.com before preaching them the following Sunday. Dr. Sherman has been widowed since the passing of his wife, Dr. Dolores E. Sherman, December 15, 2008. They had no children.